Detroit Studies in
Music Bibliography

General Editor
Bruno Nettl
University of Illinois at Urbana-Champaign

DETROIT STUDIES IN MUSIC BIBLIOGRAPHY NUMBER THIRTY-NINE

CARLO D'ORDONEZ
1734-1786
A THEMATIC CATALOG

A. Peter Brown

INFORMATION COORDINATORS
1978
DETROIT

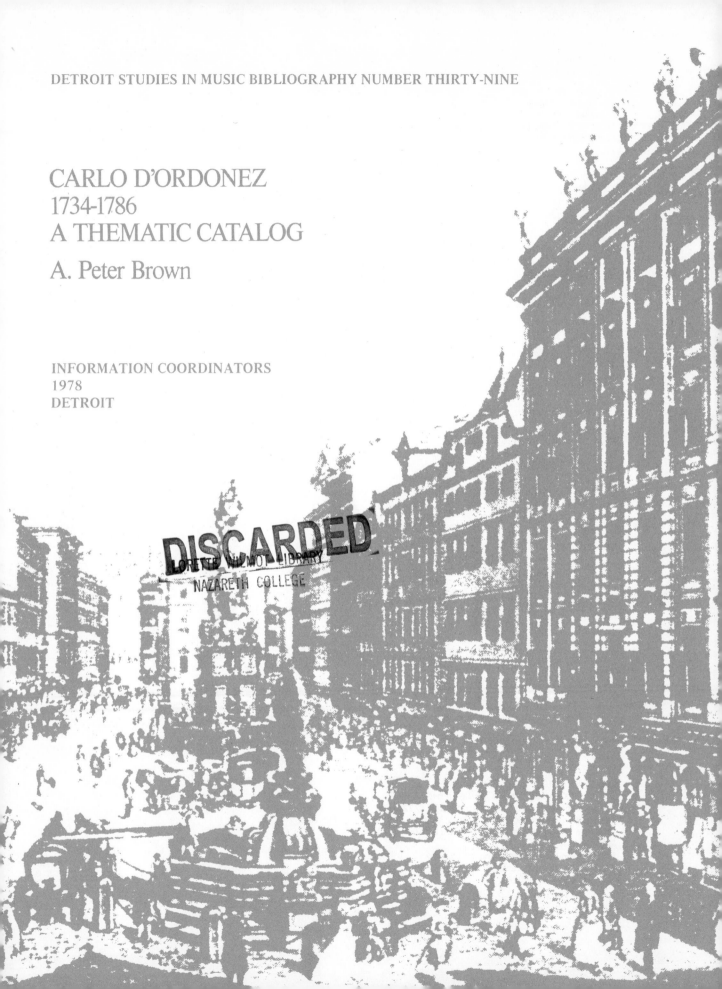

On the cover:
An enlarged signature of Ordonez.

On pages two and three:
The Graben, Vienna,
in the late Eighteenth Century.
From an engraving by
Karl Schütz, 1781.

Copyright © 1978 by A. Peter Brown
Library of Congress Catalog Card Number 78-61024
International Standard Book Number 0-911772-89-8
Designed by Vincent Kibildis
Printed and bound in the United States of America
Published by
Information Coordinators, Inc.
1435-37 Randolph Street
Detroit, Michigan 48226

CONTENTS

ILLUSTRATIONS

INTRODUCTION

CARLO D'ORDONEZ is a little known Viennese composer from the era of Haydn and Mozart. Although the importance of Ordonez's contributions to the development of the Viennese symphony and string quartet have been alluded to in a number of studies, no detailed bibliography of his output has been available. The information contained in this thematic catalog is intended to not only establish an accurate accounting of his works, but also to provide other students of the period with possible concordances for their own investigations.

As is the case with so many of the Kleinmeister active in Vienna during the mid-eighteenth century, no complete autograph survives and few of the extant works can be dated with certainty. This catalog has therefore been organized without reference to chronology. The larger organization is modeled after Anthony van Hoboken's *Joseph Haydn: Thematisch-bibliographisches Werkverzeichnis* (Mainz, 1957-1971), while within each group a system of ordering described by Jan LaRue in *Fontes Artis Musicae,* Vol. VI (1959), is employed. The works are grouped according to genre—indicated by roman numerals—beginning with the largest setting. The instrumental compositions are followed by the vocal. Within each of the instrumental groups (except Group II) the works are arranged according to tonality—beginning with C and continuing in ascending order, with major mode preceding minor; meter—beginning with the larger and moving toward the smaller metric units; and melodic activity—beginning with the smallest intervallic change, with ascending motion taking precedence over descending. Therefore, a symphony in C major in common time whose initial pitches have the least melodic motion would be designated **I: C1**. At the end of each group are listed those works of *questionable* paternity (e.g., **I/Q: C1**) and those considered *spurious* (e.g., **I/S: C1**). The letter *U* is employed if the tonality is *unknown*.

For each work a single line incipit is given. A cycle which begins with a slow movement can be distinguished from one beginning with a slow introduction by the fact that the latter will be followed on the same staff by the incipit for the main body of the movement. Minuets and their trios are also accommodated on a single staff. The probable authentic setting is given at the beginning of each entry while variants are mentioned within the appropriate catalog citation or copy entry. In Groups I and II the term "strings" indicates the standard four parts (i.e., Violin I, Violin II, Viola, and Bass), while the existence of a separate part for the cello or a second viola is indicated in parentheses; "strings a 3" refers to the standard trio sonata setting.

Under the rubric "catalogs," only those inventories of monastic collections, archives, and publishers which were in existence by the middle of the nineteenth century are included. In a number of instances, these citations are the only references to a given work.

All of the copies have been studied firsthand by the compiler except for the eight found at the following archives and libraries: Akademie der Wissenschafte in Bratislava, Fürstlich Fürstenbergische Hofbibliothek in

Donaueschingen, Universitätsbibliothek in Münster, Sächsische Landesbibliothek in Dresden, and Staatsarchiv in Rudolstadt. The locations of the copies are indicated by library sigla (see pp. 19-20) adopted by the International Musicological Society and the International Association of Music Libraries in the series *Repertoire internationale des sources musicale* (*RISM*), with the provenance when appropriate. In addition to existing shelfmarks, the generic title and any other significant inscription on the title page are noted, with those added at a later date enclosed in brackets.

The identification of unnamed scribes and the collection of information about those named caused numerous problems. It was decided to include as much information that the compiler believed to be reasonably accurate and of use to other scholars. The anonymous scribe or scribes are therefore identified as belonging to a specific copy shop or locality, by number, or in some other manner, although a more general citation (e.g., Viennese) does not preclude the possibility of preparation by one of the copyists given a more specific designation (e.g., Viennese No. 4). An index of copyists which could be identified by name or with some consistency is included. Facsimiles are reproduced for those scribes whose work was believed to be of greater than local significance. The lack of a copyist designation indicates an inability to define the sphere of his activities.

Within the watermark descriptions, a slash separates figures which are on the same sheet, but removed in space; a semicolon indicates a probable different paper. When possible, measurements in millimeters of figures and letters from their most distant vertical points are included. If the measurement occurs at the end of the description, it applies to the entire figure; if the measurement occurs after a single element, it applies to only that element. Dimensions are not given for works not traced or for watermarks cut when individual sheets were formed. Unfortunately, the state of the watermark itself, library rules and conditions, as well as changes in the compiler's approach to the problem, precluded the presentation of this data as accurately and completely as might be desirable. A complete index of watermarks is provided; those watermarks that could be dated with some certainty have been reproduced. Apart from the aforementioned copies located at the libraries not visited, the lack of a watermark description indicates the watermark was either indecipherable or not present. It should also be noted that the discrepancies in the descriptions appearing in Brown/ CHAMBER and this catalog are a result of differing approach: in Brown/CHAMBER the descriptions included collations of various letters and figures for dating purposes, while here only those elements appearing in the copy in question are offered.

Ordonez's music was not printed with the frequency with which it was copied. Many of the publications advertised in publishers' catalogs are not extant; in some cases, perhaps the advertised work was never published. Indeed, the only surviving prints—the symphony I: C9 and the six string quartets Opus 1—were both published by the little known and mysterious chez Guera of Lyon, but were also distributed in London by Longman and Broderip and Vienna by Artaria. The three modern editions are also cited (I: C10, Opus 1, and VIIa: 1).

References to a given work in the literature are also indicated in abbreviated form; full bibliographic citations are provided in the list of literature. Many of the references cited involve only mention of the work in question. Announcements, advertisements, and other references to works which could not be associated with a specific composition are presented in a separate list.

Due to the numerous spellings of the name "Carlo d'Ordonez" in the various early manuscripts listed herein, as well as in the modern literature, a brief discussion of the orthography of the name seems appropriate. Although a Spanish surname, the tilde over the "n" is not found in a single contemporary source. Indeed, the use of the tilde in modern references by H. C. Robbins Landon and others can probably be traced to Eitner's *Quellen-Lexikon.* The compiler of this catalog likewise spelled the name with a tilde until he had the opportunity to personally examine the sources. (The spelling of the surname in Brown/CHAMBER was changed by the editor of *Acta Musicologica* to conform to the house style based on *Die Musik in Geschichte und Gegenwart.*)

In addition to the problem of the tilde, there are—as might be expected—a number of variations in the spelling of the surname. The following is a list of those variants which occur five or more times in an available population from the early sources (i.e., the copies, prints, and literature up to 1812, the publication date of the Ordonez entry in Gerber's *Neues historisch-biographisches Lexikon der Tonkünstler*):

Ordonez	108
Ordeniz	15
Ordonetz	12
Ordoniz	7
Ordonitz	5
Ordenitz	5

Further evidence exists to confirm that "Ordonez" is the authentic spelling: there are two examples of the composer's signature—the title page of the *Alceste* autograph (see p. 148) and an attendance list of the Tonkünstler Societät dated 16 September 1779—and this spelling occurs in copies by a Viennese professional copyist shop (Group A) which probably had a direct connection with the composer. From all these variants we can also assume that in eighteenth-century Vienna the surname was probably not pronounced in the Spanish manner, but Germanically: ORdōnĕtz, with the stress on the initial syllable.

Regarding the Christian name, not a single extant early source provides support for the Spanish form "Carlos." The German form "Karl" ("Carl"), usually followed by the prefix "von," does occur with some frequency. However, there is a discrepancy in the spelling of the Christian name between the *Alceste* autograph and the other contemporary sources: an overwhelming preference for "Carlo d'," regardless of surname, is revealed in the sources, while "Karl v." appears on the title page of the autograph score. This writer has chosen to adopt the spelling "Carlo d'Ordonez."

———————

Our understanding of the development of the eighteenth century classical style is still comparatively incomplete. It is only from comprehensive efforts to deal with the musical sources and style development of unknown composers that a relatively secure body of facts can be gathered; thematic catalogs which supply bibliographic data are a primary requisite. It is hoped that this effort will be recognized as a contribution to the bibliographic control of this vast but still little explored repertoire.

ACKNOWLEDGMENTS

My STUDY OF ORDONEZ'S MUSIC has received support and encouragement from many quarters. A fellowship from the American Council of Learned Societies made possible twelve months of work in Europe to complete the research for this project. The compiler would like to especially thank Jan LaRue, who initially placed his materials at my disposal and willingly answered my inquiries, and H. C. Robbins Landon, who compared the entire typescript with his own files, as well as the following people who provided personal assistance:

The Abbot of Göttweig
P. Bruno Brandstetter, Melk
Dr. Paul R. Bryan, Durham
Mr. Hugh Cobbe, London
Dr. Georg Feder, Cologne
Dr. Emil Hradecký, Prague
Dr. Cari Johansson, Stockholm
Dr. István Kecskeméti, Budapest
Dr. P. Altman Kellner, Kremsmünster
Dr. Warren Kirkendale, Durham
Dr. Karl-Heinz Köhler, Berlin
Dr. Ortrun Landmann, Dresden
Frau Christa Landon, Vienna
Prof. Hermann Lang, Lambach
Dr. Jens Peter Larsen, Charlottenlund
Dr. Hedwig Mitringer, Vienna
Dr. Karl Pfannhauser, Vienna
Prof. Salvatore Pintacuda, Genoa
Dr. Pietro Puliatti, Modena
Dr. Heinz Ramge, Berlin
Dr. Jiří Sehnal, Brno
Dr. H. Watkins Shaw, London
Prof. László Somfai, Budapest
The Staff of the Musiksammlung, Österreichische Nationalbibliothek

Dr. Theodora Straková, Brno

Dr. Erich Thurmann, Münster

Dr. Alan Tyson, London

Dr. Albert Vander Linden, Brussels

Dr. Volker Volckamer, Harburg über Donauwörth

Dr. Jiří Záhola, Cesky Krumlov

I am also grateful to my wife Carol who, as usual, provided the organizational acumen which helped to bring this project to fruition.

Böhme	*Verzeichniss der neuesten Musikalien welche in der Kunst- Musik- und Instrumenten-handlung von Johann August Böhme der Börse gegenüber zu haben sind. Elfte Fortsetzung* (Hamburg, 1800). **A-Wgm**
Breitkopf	*Catalogo delle sinfonie, partite, overture, soli, duetti, trii, quattrie concerti per il violino, flauto traverso, cembalo ed altri stromenti, che si trovano in manuscritto nella officina musica di Giovanni Gottlob Breitkopf in Lipsia* (Leipzig, 1762-1765). *Supplemento I-XVI* (1766-1787). [Column citations in the text are from the reprint edition by Barry S. Brook (New York: Dover, 1966).]
Clam-Gallas	"Catalogo Delle Carte di Musica appartenenti al Sige Conte Cristiano Clam é Gallas, Da me per conservare Speer Maestro di Musica." (ca. 1810) **CS-Pnm**
Donau	"Copia Verzeichniss Nr. 12 der fürstlichen Musikalien, Pulte Instrumente . . . im Monat Junij 1804." **D-brd-DO**
Egk	"Cathalogus über die Hochfürstl. Musicalia und Instrumenten." (ca. 1759-1760) **CS-OLa**
Fuchs	"Thematisches Verzeichnis der sämtlichen Kompositionen von Joseph Haydn, zusammengestellt von Alois Fuchs, 1839." Facsimile edition by Richard Schaal (Wilhelmshaven: Heinrichshofen's Verlag, 1968).
Göttweig	"Katalogus Operum musicalium in Choro musicali Monasterii O.S.P.B. Gottwicensis R.R.D.D. Altmanno Abbate per R.D. Henricum Wondratsch p.t. chori regentem, conscriptus. Anno MDCCCXXX Tom. 1." **A-GÖ**
HBV	"J. Haydn's Verzeichniss musicalischer Werke theils eigner, theils fremder Compsition [*sic*]." **GB-Lbm**
HNV	[Haydn-Nachlass-Verzeichnis, 1809.] Archiv der Stadt Wien. **A-Wn**
Hummel	"Inventarium der Hochfürstlich Esterházyschen Kamer und Theater = Musicalien . . . 1806." **A-Ee**
Kačina	"Catalogo." (ca. 1809) **CS-Pnm**

Klosterneuburg	"Catalogus Deren auf Diesem Löbl. Stift Chor befindlichen Musicalien und Instrumenten. Verfasst von Leopold Joseph Schmidt derzeit Organist, und Chor Regent Stift Closterneuburg den 20ten 8bris 790." **A-KN**
Lambach	"Catalogus Musicalium et Instrumentorum ad Chorum Lambacensem pertinentium. Conscriptge MDCCLXIIX [1768]." **A-LA**
Melk	"Katalog von Musikalien beim Regenschoriat zu Melk 787." **A-M**
Náměšt	"Catalogo della Musica, nello qvale si trovano Sinfonie, Sestetti, Qvintetti, Qvartetti, Terzetti e Duetti, Oratorj, Operè, Cori, Psalmi, Cantate e Messe, Sonate ed Arie per il Pianoforte. Musica d'Harmonia e Diversi Concerti." (ca. 1810) **CS-Bm**
d'Ogny	"Catalogue de la Musique de Monsieur Le Comte d'Ogny." (ca. 1785) **GB-Lbm**
Osek	"Syllabus seu Catalogus perutilis non Choralia, Verum figuralia pia festivi Chori proferens artificia, quae pro felici officij habiti fine in Bacchanalijs suavioris Instar Musicae filiali ex reverentia Reverendissimo, ac Amplissimo Domino Domino Cajetano Sac: ac Exempti Ordinis Cisterciensis, Celeberrimi Monasterij B: V: Mariae de Osseco Abbati, Regni Bohemiae Praelato Dignissimo, Patri Suo Venerandissimo offert Filius obediens Fr. nomine Nivardus Sommer cognomine dictus." (1754, 1802 and 1817) **CS-Pnm**
Pirnitz	"Inventario per la musica des Grafen Thomas Vinciguerra Collalto aus Schloss Pirnitz." (ca. 1752) **CS-Bm**
Quartbuch	"Z Thematischer Cathalog verschiedener Compositionen von verschiedenen Meistern." [References here based on twentieth-century copy in **A-Wn**.]
Rajhrad	"Consignatio Musicalium id est Missarumi Offertoriorum Ariae Vesperarum . . . Antiphonarum Symphoniarum & reliquarum Parthiarum etc: pro Monasterio Rayhradensi OSB in Moravia an. 1771." **CS-Bm**
Regensburg	"Catalogus sämtlicher Hochfürstl. Thurn und Taxisch. Sinphonien." [Incipit-Katalog sämtlicher in der fürstl. Musikbibliothek vorhandenen Sinfonien, ca. 1782-1795.] **D-brd-Rtt**
Ringmacher	"Catalogo de' Soli, Duetti, Trii, Quadri, Quintetti, Partite, de' Concerti e delle Sinfonie per il Cembalo, Violino, Flauto traverso ed altri Stromenti . . . di Christiano Ulrico Ringmacher Libraio in Berolino." (1773) **B-Bc**
Sigmaringen	"Catalogus über die Sämtliche Musicalische Werck, und derselben Authorn, nach Alphabetischer Ordnung: Welche von Ihro Hochfürstl. Durchlaucht Dem Durchlauchtigsten Fürsten und Herrn Herrn Carl Friederich Erbprinzen zu Hohenzollern, Burggrafen zu Nürenberg, Grafen zu Sigmaringen und Vöhringen . . . angeschafft worden seynd. Consignirt von mir dem Expeditions Rath, und Music: Directore Schindele aº: 1766." **D-brd-SI**
Traeg	*Verzeichniss alter und neuer sowohl geschriebener als gestochener Musikalien, welche in der Kunst= und Musikalienhandlung des Johann Traeg, zu Wien, in der Singerstrasse Nr. 957. zu haben sind* (Vienna, 1799). **A-Wn**
Waldburg-Zeil	["Musikalienkataloge."] (1767-ca. 1786) **D-brd-ZL**
Westphal	*Verzeichniss derer Musicalien, welche in der Niederlage auf den grossen Bleichen bey Johann Christoph Westphal und Comp. in Hamburg in Commission zu haben sind* (Hamburg, 1782). **A-Wgm**

LIBRARY SIGLA

AUSTRIA

A-Ee	Eisenstadt, Esterházy-Archiv
A-Gd	Graz, Bibliothek des Bischöflichen Seckauer Ordinariats (Diözese Graz-Seckau)
A-GÖ	Göttweig, Benediktiner-Stift Göttweig, Musikarchiv
A-KN	Klosterneuburg, Augustiner-Chorherrenstift
A-KR	Kremsmünster, Benediktiner-Stift Kremsmünster, Musikarchiv
A-LA	Lambach, Benediktiner-Stift Lambach
A-M	Melk an der Donau, Benediktiner-Stift Melk
A-Ssp	Salzburg, St. Peter (Erzstift oder Benediktiner-Erzabtei), Musikarchiv
A-SCH	Schlägl, Prämonstratenser-Stift Schlägl
A-SF	St. Florian, Augustiner-Chorherrenstift
A-ST	Stams, Zisterzienserstift
A-Wgm	Wien, Gesellschaft der Musikfreunde
A-Wmi	Wien, Musikwissenschaftliches Institut der Universität Wien
A-Wn	Wien, Österreichische Nationalbibliothek, Musiksammlung
A-Wpfannhauser	Wien, Privatbibliothek Dr. Karl Pfannhauser
A-Wst	Wien, Stadtbibliothek, Musiksammlung

BELGIUM

B-Bc	Bruxelles, Conservatoire Royal de Musique, Bibliothèque

CZECHOSLOVAKIA

CS-Bm	Brno, Moravské múzeum-hud. hist. oddělěni
CS-BRnm	Bratislava, Slovenské národné múzeum, hudobné oddělenie
CS-BRsa	Bratislava, Státný slovensky ústredný archív
CS-K	Český Krumlov, póbočka Stát. archívu Třeboň Hudební sbírka Schwarzenberg-Oettingen Svozy
CS-KRm	Kroměříž, Umělecko-historické múzeum
CS-Mms	Martin, Matica slovenská, Literárny archív
CS-OLa	Olomouc, Státní archív - Arcibiskupská sbírka
CS-Pnm	Praha, Národní múzeum, hudební oddelění

WEST GERMANY

D-brd-B	Berlin, Staatsbibliothek (Stiftung Preussischer Kulturbesitz)
D-brd-DO	Donaueschingen, Fürstlich Fürstenbergische Hofbibliothek
D-brd-HR	Harburg über Donauwörth, Fürstlich Öttingen-Wallerstein'sche Bibliothek, Schloss Harburg
D-brd-MÜu	Münster, Universitätsbibliothek
D-brd-Rtt	Regensburg, Fürstlich Thurn und Taxis'sche Hofbibliothek
D-brd-SI	Sigmaringen, Fürstlich Hohenzollernsche Hofbibliothek
D-brd-ZL	Zeil (Bayern), Fürstlich Waldburg-Zeil'sches Archiv

EAST GERMANY

D-ddr-Bds	Berlin, Deutsche Staatsbibliothek, Musikabteilung
D-ddr-Dlb	Dresden, Sächsische Landesbibliothek, Musikabteilung
D-ddr-RU1	Rudolstadt, Staatsarchiv

FRANCE

F-Lm	Lille, Bibliothèque municipale

GREAT BRITAIN

GB-Cu	Cambridge, University Library
GB-Lbm	London, British Museum
GB-Lcm	London, Royal College of Music

HUNGARY

H-Bn	Budapest, Országos Széchényi Könyvtár (National Széchényi Library)
H-KE	Keszthely, Helikon Castle Museum

ITALY

I-Fc	Firenze, Biblioteca del Conservatorio di Musica "L. Cherubini"
I-Gi(l)	Genova, Istituto musicale (Biblioteca del Liceo Musicale "Paganini")
I-MOe	Modena, Biblioteca Estense
I-Nc	Napoli, Biblioteca del Conservatorio di Musica S. Pietro a Maiella

SWEDEN

S-Sk	Stockholm, Kungliga Biblioteket
S-Skma	Stockholm, Kungliga Musikaliska Akademiens Biblioteket

UNITED STATES OF AMERICA

US-NYp	New York, New York Public Library at Lincoln Center
US-Wc	Washington, D.C., Library of Congress, Music Division

LITERATURE

ATA   *Allgemeine Theater Almanach* (Vienna).

Barrett-Ayres/HAYDN   Reginald Barrett-Ayres. *Joseph Haydn and the String Quartet.* London, 1974.

Bartha/BRIEFE   Dénes Bartha. *Joseph Haydn: Gesammelte Briefe und Aufzeichnungen.* Kassel, 1965.

Bartha-Somfai/HAYDN   Dénes Bartha and László Somfai. *Haydn als Opernkapellmeister.* Budapest, 1960.

Benton/PLEYEL   Rita Benton. *Ignace Pleyel: A Thematic Catalogue.* New York, 1977.

BESCHREIBUNG   Beschreibung des hochfürstlichen Schlosses Esterháss im Königreiche Ungern. Pressburg, 1784.

Brown/CHAMBER   A. Peter Brown. "The Chamber Music with Strings of Carlos d'Ordoñez: A Bibliographic and Stylistic Study." *Acta Musicologica,* XLVI/2 (1974), 222-72.

Brown/INTRODUCTION   A. Peter Brown. "An Introduction to the Life and Works of Carlo d'Ordonez." *Music East and West: Essays in Honor of Walter Kaufmann,* edited by Thomas Noblitt, forthcoming.

Brown/QUARTETS   A. Peter Brown. "Structure and Style in the String Quartets of Carlos d'Ordoñez." *International Musicological Society. Report of the Eleventh Congress, Copenhagen 1972,* Vol. I, pp. 314-24. Copenhagen, 1974.

Bryan/VANHAL   Paul R. Bryan. "The Symphonies of Johann Vanhal." Unpublished dissertation, University of Michigan, 1955.

DTB   *Denkmäler der Tonkunst in Bayern.*

Geiringer/HAYDN   Karl Geiringer. *Haydn. A Creative Life in Music.* Berkeley, 1968.

Gerber/1792   Ernst Ludwig Gerber. *Historisch-biographisches Lexicon der Tonkünstler,* Vol. II. Leipzig, 1792.

Gericke/ MUSIKALIENHANDEL	Hannelore Gericke. *Der Wiener Musikalienhandel von 1700 bis 1778.* Graz, 1960.
Hadamowsky/ LEOPOLDSTADT	Franz Hadamowsky. *Das Theater in der Wiener Leopoldstadt 1781-1860.* Vienna, 1934.
Hanslick/ VIRTUOSENCONCERTE	Eduard Hanslick. "Wiener Virtuosenconcerte im vorigen Jahrhundert." *Jahrbuch der Vereine Landeskunde von Niederoesterreich* (Vienna). 1868.
Harich/ESTERHÁZY	Janos Harich. "Esterházy-zenetörténet." Typescript, National Széchényi Library, Budapest.
Johansson/FRENCH	Cari Johansson. *French Music Publishers' Catalogues of the Second Half of the Eighteenth Century.* Stockholm, 1955.
Kirkendale/FUGE	Warren Kirkendale. *Fuge und Fugato in der Kammermusik des Rokoko und der Klassik.* Tutzing, 1966.
Krebs/DITTERSDORF	Carl Krebs. *Dittersdorfiana.* Berlin, 1900.
Kucaba/WAGENSEIL	John Kucaba. "The Symphonies of Georg Christoph Wagenseil." Unpublished dissertation, Boston University, 1967.
Landon/CCLN	H. C. Robbins Landon. *The Collected Correspondence and London Notebooks of Joseph Haydn.* London, 1959.
Landon/DOUBTFUL	H. C. Robbins Landon. "Doubtful and Spurious Quartets and Quintets Attributed to Haydn." *The Music Review,* XVIII/2 (1957), 213-21.
Landon/HAYDN	H. C. Robbins Landon. *Haydn Symphonies.* (B.B.C. Music Guides.) London, 1966.
Landon/MARIONETTE	H. C. Robbins Landon. "Haydn's Marionette Operas and the Repertoire of the Marionette Theatre at Esterház Castle." *The Haydn Yearbook,* I (1962), 111-93.
Landon/MGG	H. C. Robbins Landon. "Carlos d'Ordoñez." *Die Musik in Geschichte und Gegenwart,* Vol. X, cols. 194-96. Kassel, 1962.
Landon/OPERA 1 AND 2	H. C. Robbins Landon. "On Haydn's Quartets of Opera 1 and 2." *The Music Review,* XIII/3 (1952), 181-86.
Landon/PROBLEMS	H. C. Robbins Landon. "Problems of Authenticity in Eighteenth-Century Music." *Instrumental Music,* edited by D. Hughes, pp. 31-56. Boston, 1959.
Landon/SUPPLEMENT	H. C. Robbins Landon. *The Symphonies of Joseph Haydn: Supplement.* London, 1961.
Landon/SYMPHONIES	H. C. Robbins Landon. *The Symphonies of Joseph Haydn.* London, 1955.
Larsen/DHK	Jens Peter Larsen. *Drei Haydn Kataloge in Faksimile.* Copenhagen, 1941.

Larsen/HÜB	Jens Peter Larsen. *Die Haydn-Überlieferung.* Copenhagen, 1939.
Larsen/QUARTBUCH	Jens Peter Larsen. "Haydn und das kleine Quartbuch." *Acta Musicologica,* VII/3 (1935), 111-23.
LaRue/BACKGROUND	Jan LaRue. "The Background of the Classical Symphony." *The Symphony,* edited by Ursula Rauchhaupt, pp. 99-109. London, 1973.
LaRue/MGG	Jan LaRue. "Symphonie, Wien." *Die Musik in Geschichte und Gegenwart,* Vol. XII, cols. 1810-19. Kassel, 1965.
Michtner/BURGTHEATER	Otto Michtner. Das Alte Burgtheater als Opernbühne. Vienna, 1970.
Morales/COBBETT'S	Pedro G. Morales. "Ordoñez, Cárlos." *Cyclopedic Survey of Chamber Music,* compiled and edited by Walter Wilson Cobbett, Vol. II, p. 201. London, 1929.
Múdra/ SPIŠSKÁ KAPITULA	Darina Múdra. *Die Musik in Spišská Kapitula in der Zeit der Klassik.* Bratislava, 1971.
Pohl/DENKSCHRIFT	Carl Ferdinand Pohl. *Denkschrift aus Anlass des 100 jähr. Bestehens der Tonkünstler-Societät.* Vienna, 1871.
Pohl/HAYDN	Carl Ferdinand Pohl. *Joseph Haydn,* Vols. I and II. Berlin, 1875 and 1882.
Pollheimer/PAUERSBACH	Klaus M. Pollheimer. "Karl Michael (Joseph) von Pauersbach (1737-1802)." *Jahrbuch für österreichische Kulturgeschichte,* III (1973), 34 ff.
PZ	*Pressburger Zeitung.*
Scholz-Michelitsch/ WAGENSEIL	Helga Scholz-Michelitsch. *Das Orchester- und Kammermusikwerk von Georg Christoph Wagenseil. Thematischer Katalog.* (Tabulae Musicae Austriacae, Vol. VI.) Vienna, 1972.
Scott/ OPUS TWO AND THREE	Marion M. Scott. "Haydn's Opus Two and Opus Three." *Proceedings of the Royal Musical Association,* LXI (1934-35), 1-19.
Sehnal/EGK	Jiří Sehnal. "Das Musikinventar des Olmützer Bischofs Leopold Egk aus dem Jahre 1760 als Quelle vorklassischer Instrumentalmusik." *Archiv für Musikwissenschaft,* XXIX/4 (1972), 285-317.
Sehnal/HAMILTON	Jiří Sehnal. "Die Musikkapelle des Olmützer Bischofs Maximilian Hamilton." *Die Musikforschung,* XXIV/4 (1971), 411-17.
Sonnleithner/ MATERIALIEN	Leopold Sonnleithner. "Materialien zur Geschichte der Oper und des Ballets in Wien. IIIte Abtheilung: Das Theater in der Leopoldstadt und das Theater am Franz-Josephs Quai." Manuscript, Gesellschaft der Musikfreunde in Wien.
Unverricht/TRIOS	Hubert Unverricht. *Geschichte des Streichtrios.* Tutzing, 1969.
Walin/SINFONIK	Stig Walin. *Beiträge zur Geschichte der Schwedischen Sinfonik.* Stockholm, 1941.
WD	*Wienerisches Diarium - Wiener Zeitung.*
Wellesz-Sternfeld/ SYMPHONY	Egon Wellesz and F. W. Sternfeld. "The Early Symphony." *The New Oxford History of Music,* Vol. III, pp. 366-433. London, 1973.

Group I
SYMPHONIES

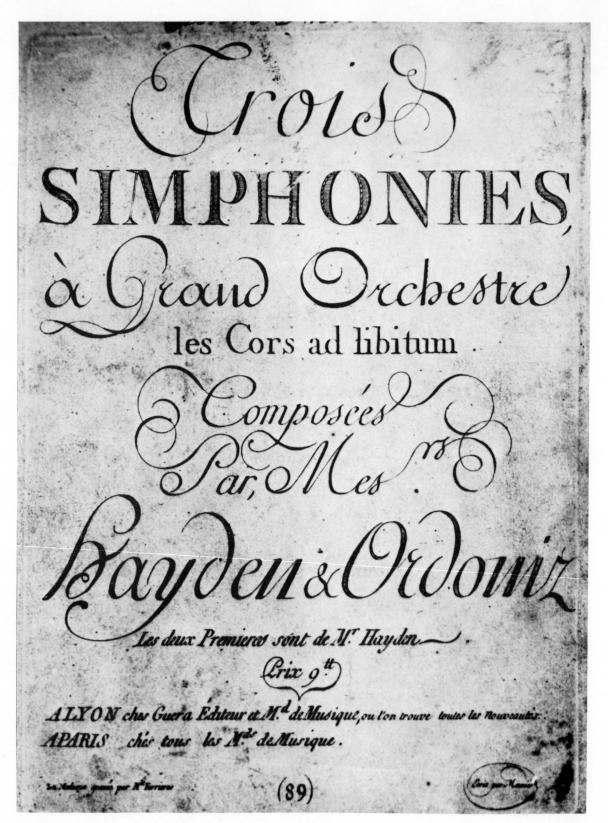

Title page from Guera print of *Trois Simphonies . . . Par Mesrs. Hayden & Ordoniz* **(I: C9)**

I: C1 STRINGS

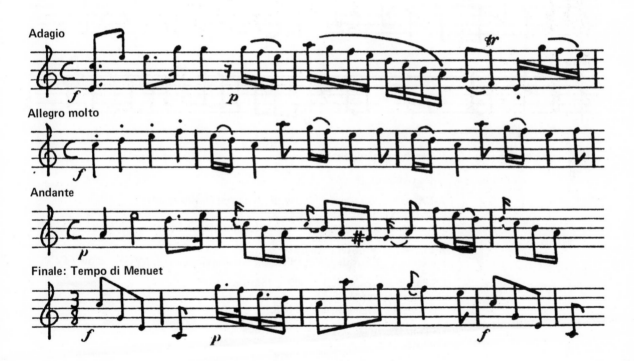

Adagio

Allegro molto

Andante

Finale: Tempo di Menuet

Catalog Entry   Göttweig p. 890, no. 1; dated 1756 P. Leandri

Copies   **A-GÖ** "Sinfonia . . ." (with 2 horns)
Copyist Leandri

CS-Pnm (Doksy) XXXIV-B-144. "Sinfonia . . ."
Copyists Group A
Watermark Eagle (broken) / BVT[19] inside rectangular frame[24] (?-broken)[64]

D-brd-HR III, 4-½, 2°, 1064. "Sinfonia . . . [de Donnersperg]" (with 2 horns)
Copyist Viennese?
Watermark Eagle / IGS

Literature	Brown/CHAMBER pp. 234-36, 243
	Brown/INTRODUCTION
	LaRue/BACKGROUND p. 107
	Wellesz-Sternfeld/SYMPHONY p. 401
Remarks	The horn parts at **A-GÖ** and **D-brd-HR** are not the same.

I: C2   STRINGS, SOLO VIOLIN, SOLO CELLO, 2 OBOES, 2 HORNS, 2 CLARINI AND TIMPANI

Catalog Entry	Regensburg Ordonez No. 3
Copies	**A-Gd** (Aussee) (lost)
	A-LA 69. "Sinfonia . . ." (without clarini and timpani)
	Copyist Viennese?
	Watermark 3 crescents / primitive flower with $\frac{CS}{C}$ below
	B-BC W.7779 (title page lost)
	Watermark Fleur de lys[65], shield on bottom (broken)[55] LVG[16] below / IV[16]
	CS-Pnm (Osek) XXXII-A-342. "Sinfonia . . ."
	Copyists Group A
	Watermark Eagle (broken) / IGS
	CS-Pnm (Pachta) XXII-E9. "Sinfonia . . ."
	Copyists Group A
	Watermark Eagle (broken) / IGS
	D-brd-Rtt Ordonez No. 3. "Sinfonia . . ." (without clarini and timpani)
	Copyist Viennese No. 6?
	Watermark Crescent/six-pointed(?) star with circle inside
Conflicting Attributions	Joseph Haydn. See Hob. I: C13
	A similar incipit is found in a symphony attributed to both Dittersdorf and Vanhal.
Literature	Bryan/VANHAL p. 294
	Landon/PROBLEMS p. 36
	Landon/SYMPHONIES p. 801, no. 13

I: C3 STRINGS, 2 OBOES, 2 HORNS, 2 CLARINI AND TIMPANI

Copy	**CS-KRm** IV.B.18. "Partitta Solenne . . . [766]"
	Copyist local?
Literature	Brown/INTRODUCTION
	Gerber/1792

I: C4 STRINGS, 2 CLARINI AND TIMPANI

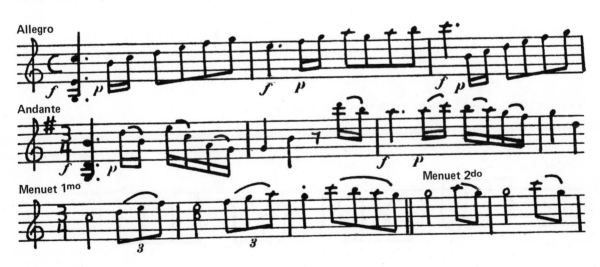

Catalog Entry	Rajhrad
Copy	**CS-Bm** (Rajhrad) A.14.299 (clarini and timpani parts lost). "Symphonia . . ."
	Copyist local

I: C5 STRINGS, 2 OBOES, 2 HORNS, 2 CLARINI AND TIMPANI

Allegro

Andante alla Francesa

Allegro

Catalog Entry	Quartbuch II, p. 40, no. 22
Copies	**CS-Pnm** (Osek) XXXIII-E-78. "Serenade . . ."
	Copyist local
	I-MOe D.280. "Sinfonia . . ."
	Copyists Group A
	Watermark Crossed swords (?) / coat of arms (?) / MM (or MV or MW?)

I: C6 STRINGS, 2 OBOES, 2 HORNS, 2 CLARINI AND TIMPANI

Allegro

Catalog Entries	Göttweig p. 891, no. 7
	Quartbuch II, p. 40, no. 25

I: C7   STRINGS (2 VIOLAS AND CELLO), 2 OBOES AND 2 HORNS

Copies   **A-Wn**   S.m.3712. "Sinfonia . . ."
              Copyist   Viennese No. 4
              Watermarks   Fleur de lys (broken)[53] ; Crossed keys or crossed swords[75]

              CS-K   45a. "Sinfonia . . ."
              Copyist   Viennese?
              Watermark   Eagle with crown on top[112] / IHE (broken)[22]

              I-Fc (Pitti)   D.V.84. "Sinfonia . . ."
              Copyist   Viennese No. 7
              Watermark   3 crescents, decreasing size[35], REAL (broken)[26] below /
                        baldachin (broken)[43] with GF (broken)[33] below

I: C8   STRINGS, 2 OBOES, 2 HORNS, 2 CLARINI AND TIMPANI

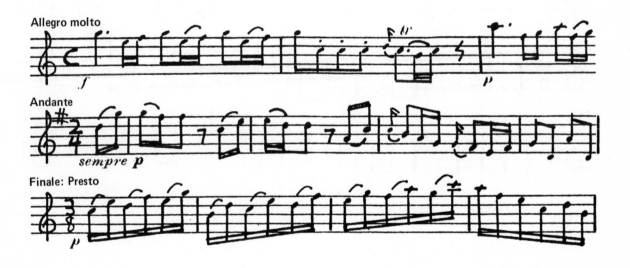

Catalog Entries	Klosterneuburg p. 81
	Rajhrad p. 156, no. 64

Copies **CS-KRm** IV.A.235. "Sinfonia . . ."
Copyist Viennese?
Watermark Flower with curled root (?-broken)[80], B_D (broken)[21] below

CS-Mms (Marianka) 17. "Sinfonia . . . Ex musicalium Prof. Lang"
Copyist local

CS-Pnm (Doksy) XXXIV-B-153. "Sinfonia . . ."
Copyists Group A
Watermark 3 crescents / anchor[53], W[30] below

CS-Pnm (Pachta) XXII-E-12. "Sinfonia . . ."
Copyists Group A
Watermark 2 human figures facing each other, plant in middle (?-broken),
    ALLEMODEPAPEIR (?) below (broken)

I-MOe D.279. "Sinfonia . . ."
Copyists Group A
Watermark 2 human figures facing each other, plant in middle (?-broken),
    ALLEMODEPAPEIR (?) below (broken)

Keyboard Arrangement **CS-KRm** II.A.242. "Sinfonia . . ."
Copyist local?
Watermark 3 crescents, decreasing size (center one with crook) / A[25] with ?
    above (broken) / incomplete letter (?)

I: C9 STRINGS, 2 OBOES, 2 HORNS, 2 CLARINI AND TIMPANI

Catalog Entries	Clam-Gallas Sinfonia, Ordenetz No. 6
	Göttweig p. 893, no. 17; dated 1780 P. Marianus
	Quartbuch II, p. 40, no. 27

SIMPHONIA

PER

Due Violini, Due Oboi,

Due Corni, Due Clarini,

Tympano, Viola,

E Basso doppio.

Composta

Del Signore

DE ORDONIZ.

n:º I.

Prezzo 2ˡᵗ 8ᶜ

A LYON

Chez Guera Editeur et Mᵈ. de Musique Place des Terreaux

A Paris au Bureau du Journal de Musique rue Montmartre.

Aux adresses Ordinaires de Musique.

Gravé par Charpentier fils.

28

Title page from Guera print of Symphony I: C9

Beginning of 1st Violin part from Guera print of Symphony I: C9

Copies	**CS-Mms** (Svaty Jur) 86. "Sinfonia . . . In Festo 3 Regum"

Copyist   local?

CS-Pnm (Clam-Gallas) XLII-B-229. "Sinfonia . . ."
Copyist   Viennese
Watermarks   Horse (?-broken)[86] / Fleur de lys (broken)[71]; 3 crescents, decreasing size[39], bow with arrow through it (broken)[69] below; Ornament with crown on top[152] and $\frac{AZ\,28}{C23}$ inside (broken)

CS-Pnm (Doksy) XXXIV-B-155. "Sinfonia . . ."
Copyist   Viennese
Watermark   Baldachin with crescent on top[67] / CF (?)[31]

CS-Pnm (Horšovský Týn) XLI.A.121. "Sinfonia . . ."
Copyist   Viennese
Watermark   Baldachin with crescent on top / CF (?)

I-Gi(l) (Assereto?) SS.A.2.12.(H.7). "Sinfonia . . ."
Copyists   Group B
Watermark   3 crescents, decreasing size[40] / GR_DG (?-broken)[32]

Prints   SIMPHONIA / PER / Due Violini, Due Oboi, / Due Corni, Due Clarini, / Tympano, Viola, / É Basso doppio. / Composta / Del Signor / DE ORDONIZ / No. I / Prezzo 2tt 8f / A LYON / Chez Guera Editeur et Md. de Musique Place des Terreaux / A PARIS au Bureau du Journal de Musique rue Montmartre / Aux adresses Ordinaires de Musique. / Gravé par Charpentier fils. / 28.
Announcements   *Almanach Musical* (Paris) for 1778, p. 119; Breitkopf catalog for 1778, col. 630; *Mercure de France,* September 1777; Westphal catalog for 1782, p. 16
Locations   **A-SF**, **F-Lm**, **US-Wc**

Trois / SIMPHONIES / à / Grand Orchestre / les Cors ad libitum. / Composées / Par Mesrs. / Hayden & Ordoniz / Les deux Premieres sont de Mr. Hayden. / Prix 9tt / A LYON ches Guera Editeur et Md. de Musique, ou l'on trouve toutes les Nouveautés. / A PARIS chés tous les Mds. de Musique. / La Musique gravée par Mle Ferrieres Ecrit par Meunier / (89)
Location   **GB-Cu**
Remarks   Haydn Symphonies Hob. I: 80 and 81

Literature   Brown / INTRODUCTION

I: C10   STRINGS, 2 OBOES, 2 HORNS AND 2 CHOIRS OF 2 CLARINI AND TIMPANI

Catalog Entries	Clam-Gallas Sinfonia, Ordenetz No. 5
	Quartbuch II, p. 40, no. 24

Copies   **CS-Pnm** (Clam-Gallas)   XLII-A-170. "Sinfonia . . ." (with additional parts
   for 2 flutes)
Copyists   Viennese? and Speer
Watermark   3 crescents, decreasing size[32] / primitive flower[17] with $\frac{CG}{C}$ (?) below

CS-Pnm (Doksy)   XXXIV-B-137. "Sinfonia . . ."
Copyist   Viennese?
Watermark   3 crescents with double borders, decreasing size[40] / small horn[18] /
   HF / star

I-Fc (Pitti)   D.V.84. "Sinfonia . . ."
Copyist   Viennese No. 7
Watermark   Baldachin with crescent on top[68], GF[37] below / ornament with
   3 six-pointed stars inside (broken)[164]

I-MOe   D.289. "Sinfonia . . ."
Copyists   Group A
Watermarks   3 crescents, decreasing size[32], M (?-broken)[18] below / AS[24];
   Ornament (?) with $\frac{FA}{G}$ below

Modern Edition	Edited by H. C. R. Landon. Vienna: Universal Edition, 1972. 25A016
	(Academia Musical 16)
Literature	Brown/INTRODUCTION
	Landon/PROBLEMS p. 35

I: C11   STRINGS, 2 OBOES AND 2 HORNS

Catalog Entry	Quartbuch II, p. 40, no. 28
Copy	**B-Bc** W.7779. "Sinfonia . . ."
	Watermark Fleur de lys[65], shield on bottom (broken)[55], LVG[16] below / IV[16]

I:C12 STRINGS, 2 OBOES, 2 HORNS, 2 CLARINI AND TIMPANI

Catalog Entries	Göttweig p. 891, no. 6 Sigmaringen Ordonez No. 4
Copies	**D-ddr-Rul** (Rudolstadt Hofkapell) 07. "Sinfonia . . ." *Copyist* Viennese?
	I-MOe D.603. "Sinfonia . . ." *Copyists* Group A *Watermark* 3 crescents, decreasing size[32], M(?-broken)[18] below / AS[24]
Literature	Landon/PROBLEMS p. 35

I: C13 STRINGS, 2 OBOES AND 2 HORNS

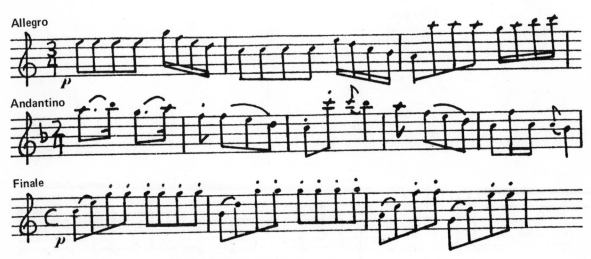

Copy	**I-MOe** E.172. "Sinfonia . . ." *Copyist* Schmutzer *Watermark* double chain lines (otherwise indecipherable)
Literature	Brown/CHAMBER p. 226 Landon/HAYDN p. 9

I: C14   STRINGS, 2 OBOES, 2 HORNS, 2 CLARINI AND TIMPANI

Catalog Entries	Quartbuch II, p. 40, no. 26
	Traeg 1799
Copies	**CS-KRm** IV.A.234. "Sinfonia . . . Ex rebus Marschalek"
	Copyist local
	Watermark Coat of arms (broken)[112] / IEW (broken)[18]
	CS-KRm (Piaristen) A.2158. "Sinfonia . . ."
	Copyist local
	Watermark Coat of arms (broken)[140]
	I-Fc (Pitti) D.V.83. "Sinfonia . . ."
	Copyist Viennese No. 7
	Watermark Baldachin with crescent on top[68], GF[37] below / ornament with 3 six-pointed stars inside (broken)[164]
Literature	Brown/INTRODUCTION

I: D1   STRINGS, 2 FLUTES (IN ANDANTE), 2 OBOES, 2 HORNS, 2 CLARINI AND TIMPANI

3

Copy	**CS-KRm** IV.A.233. "Sinfonia . . ."
	Copyists Group A
	Watermark 2 human figures facing each other, plant in middle(?-broken), ALLEMODEPAPEIR(?) below(broken)
Literature	Brown/INTRODUCTION

I: D2 STRINGS (WITH CELLO), 2 OBOES AND 2 HORNS

Catalog Entry	Lambach p. 304
Copies	**A-LA** 70. "Sinfonia . . ."
	Copyist local?
	Watermark Coat of arms with crown on top[74] / H(?) R(broken)[20]
	CS-Pnm (Doksy) XXXIV-B-181. "Sinfonia . . ."
	Copyists Group A
	Watermark Eagle(broken)[80] / IGS[14]
	CS-Pnm (Pachta) XXII-E-10. "Sinfonia . . ."
	Copyists Group A
	Watermark Eagle(broken) / IGS
	D-brd-B (Stift Heggbach) Mus.ms.16365. "Symphonia in C . . ." with the following Menuet between the Andante and Finale
	Copyist local?
	Watermark Coat of arms(broken)[80]

I: D3   STRINGS (WITH CELLO), 2 OBOES AND 2 HORNS

Copy	**I-MOe** E.170. "Sinfonia..."
	Copyist Schmutzer
	Watermark double chain lines
Literature	Brown/CHAMBER p. 226

I: D4   STRINGS

Catalog Entry	Sigmaringen Ordonez No. 1 ("Synfonia")
Copy	**CS-Pnm** (Doksy) XXXIV-B-145. "Sinfonia..."
	Copyists Group A
	Watermark 3 crescents / anchor[53], W[30] below

I: D5 STRINGS (WITH 2 VIOLAS AND CELLO), SOLO VIOLIN, SOLO CELLO, 2 OBOES, 2 HORNS, 2 CLARINI AND TIMPANI

Catalog Entry	Klosterneuburg p. 83
Copy	**I-MOe** D.292. "Sinfonia Solenne . . ."
	Copyists Group A
Literature	Brown/INTRODUCTION
	Gerber/1792

I: D6 STRINGS (WITH CELLO), 2 OBOES, BASSOON AND 2 HORNS

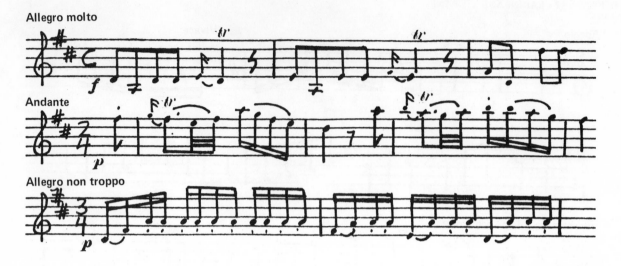

Catalog Entry	Rajhrad p. 166, no. 157

Copies **A-Wgm** XIII/1300 (old VI/1300). "Sinfonia . . ."
Copyist Viennese No. 4
Watermarks Baldachin with GF below; Crossed swords (broken)

A-Wn S.m.3713. "Sinfonia . . ."
Copyist Viennese No. 4
Watermarks Eagle, I HELLER(?); Fleur de lys (broken)[53]

CS-Bm Rajhrad A.14.298. "Sinfonia . . . Procuravit P. Maurus Reg: Chori 1779"
Copyist local
Watermark Fleur de lys[62] / ₵ (?)[43]

CS-K 45b. "Sinfonia . . ."
Copyist Viennese?
Watermark Eagle with crown on top[112] / IHE(broken)[22]

I: D7 STRINGS, 2 OBOES, 2 HORNS (OR 2 CLARINI), 2 CLARINI AND TIMPANI

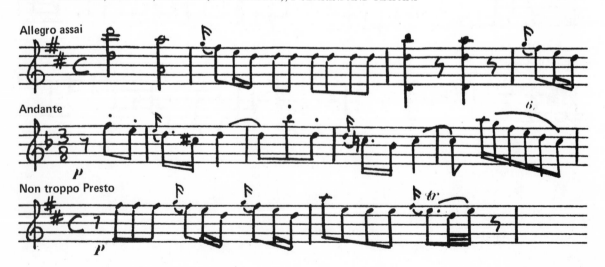

Catalog Entries	Gottweig p. 189, no. 5 (with 2 horns) Klosterneuburg p. 81 Quartbuch II, p. 45, no. 21
Copies	**A-LA** 73. "Symphonia . . ." (with 4 clarini) *Copyist* Viennese? *Watermark* Baldachin with GF below / ornament with 3 six-pointed stars inside and crescent on top

A-W Pfannhauser (Kirche am Hof)   "Sinfonia . . . [1777]" (with 2 horns)
Copyist   Viennese? A^{25}
Watermark   3 crescents, decreasing size[38] /   H F[31]
                                  R E A L[21]

A-Wmi [lost?]   (with 4 clarini)

CS-Pnm (Doksy)   XXXIV-B-154   (title page lost; with 2 horns)
Copyists   Group A
Watermarks   3 crescents / anchor[53], W[30] below; 3 crescents, M below / coat of arms

D-ddr-Rul (Rudolstadt Hofkapell)   010.   "Sinfonia . . ." (with 2 horns)
Copyist   Viennese?

Literature	Brown/INTRODUCTION

I: D8   STRINGS AND 2 HORNS

Catalog Entries	Breitkopf 1774, col. 523 Lambach p. 304
Copies	**A-LA** 68. "Sinfonia . . ." *Copyist* local? *Watermark* Lion (?) on hind legs[109], forelegs on oval with $_A{}^F{}_W{}^{20}{}^{18}$ inside (broken)

CS-Pnm (Doksy)   XXXIV-B-178.   "Sinfonia . . ."
Copyists   Group A
Watermark   Eagle (broken)[80] / IGS[14]

Conflicting Attribution	Ignaz Holzbauer. **CS-Pnm** (Doksy) XXXIV-D-35. "Sinfonia . . ."
Remarks	Of those symphonies with conflicting attributions which are considered authentic, I: D8 is the least stylistically convincing.

I: D9   STRINGS a 3, SOLO VIOLA AND SOLO CELLO

Catalog Entry	Quartbuch I, p. 15, no. 10
Copies	**CS-Pnm** (Osek) XXXII-A-562. "Sinfonia . . ." *Copyist* local
	I-MOe D.284. "Sinfonia . . ." *Copyists* Group A *Watermark* 2 human figures facing each other, plant in middle (?-broken), ALLEMODEPAPEIR (?) below (broken)

I: D10   STRINGS, 2 OBOES AND 2 HORNS

Catalog Entry	Regensburg Ordonez No. 1
	CS-Pnm (Osek) XXXII-A-345. "Sinfonia . . ." *Copyist* Joseph Los
	D-brd-Rtt Ordonez No. 1. "Sinfonia . . ." *Copyist* local? *Watermark* 4 with anchor bottom[63], ASF (?)[27] below / ML (broken)[23]
Literature	Landon/HAYDN p. 9

I: E♭1   STRINGS, 2 OBOES AND 2 HORNS

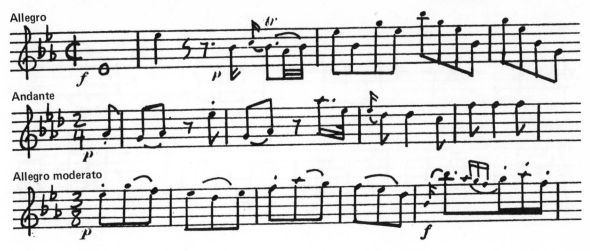

Catalog Entries	Breitkopf 1775, col. 563
	Osek O No. 27
	Quartbuch II, p. 49, no. 18

Copies	**A-Wgm** (Carrara) XIII/6376. "Sinfonia . . ." (only first and second movements, in reversed order)

Copyist Viennese No. 4
Watermark 3 crescents (lower one broken) arranged ⌢⌢ / wheel with baldachin on top, AFC[34] below

CS-Pnm (Doksy) XXXIV-B-183. "Sinfonia . . ."
Copyists Group A
Watermark 3 crescents, decreasing size[32] / primitive flower[17] with $\frac{CS^{23}}{C(?)}$[18] below

D-ddr-Rul (Rudolstadt Hofkapell) 09. "Sinfonia . . ."
Copyist Viennese?

I-Fc (Pitti) D.V.84. "Sinfonia . . ."
Copyist Viennese No. 7
Watermark Baldachin with crescent on top[68], GF[37] below / ornament with 3 six-pointed stars inside (broken)[164]

Literature	Brown/CHAMBER p. 225
	Brown/INTRODUCTION

Remarks	The two-movement version at **A-Wgm** was perhaps for liturgical use.

I: E♭2   STRINGS

[Allegro]

Catalog Entry	Egk
Literature	Sehnal/EGK p. 312

I: E♭3   STRINGS, 2 OBOES AND 2 HORNS

Copies	**B-Bc** L.H.W.7779. "Sinfonia . . ."	
	Watermark Coat of arms of two circles, right with cross, crown on top[73] / BVBG(?)	
	CS-Mms (Kremnica) 49/1. "Symphonia . . ."	
	CS-Pnm (Doksy) XXXIV-B-173. "Sinfonia . . ."	
	Copyists Group A	
	Watermark Eagle (broken)[80] / IGS[14]	
	I-Gi(l) (Assereto?) SS.A.2.12.(H.7). "Sinfonia . . ."	
	Copyists Group B	
	Watermark Bird[62] / ꙅC[23]	
Literature	Brown/INTRODUCTION	

I: E♭4   STRINGS, 2 OBOES AND 2 HORNS

Copies   **CS-Pnm** (Doksy) XXXIV-B-176. "Sinfonia . . ."
Copyists Group A
Watermark 3 crescents, A below

             CS-Pnm (Osek) XXXII-A-343. "Sinfonia . . ."
Copyists Group A
Watermark Eagle(broken) / IGS

             CS-Pnm (Pachta) XXII-E-7. "Sinfonia . . ."
Copyists Group A
Watermark Eagle(broken) / IGS

             I-Gi(l) (Assereto?) SS.A.2.12.(H.7). "Sinfonia . . ."
Copyists Group B
Watermark Bird[62] / $\supset$C[23]

I: E$^\flat$5 STRINGS, 2 OBOES AND 2 HORNS

Copies   **CS-KRm** IV.A.231. "Sinfonia . . ."
Copyists Group A
Watermark 2 human figures facing each other, plant in middle (?-broken),
         ALLEMODEPAPEIR(?) below (broken)

             CS-Pnm (Pachta) XXII-E-8. "Sinfonia . . ."
Copyists Group A
Watermark ADLER(?)[30], IPR(?)[32] below, indecipherable object above (broken)

             I-MOe D.287. "Sinfonia . . ."
Copyists Group A
Watermark Angel (holding scales in left hand?)[92], OM at feet, RP(?)[15]
         below (broken)

I: E1   STRINGS, 2 OBOES AND 2 HORNS

Copies	**CS-Pnm** (Doksy) XXXIV-B-150. "Sinfonia . . ."
	Copyist Viennese?
	Watermark 3 crescents, decreasing size, P^{19} below / AS(?)
	I-Gi(l) (Assereto?) SS.A.2.12.(H.7). "Sinfonia . . ."
	Copyists Group B
	Watermark Bird^{62} / $\supset C^{23}$
Literature	Brown/INTRODUCTION

I: E2   STRINGS, 2 OBOES AND 2 HORNS

Copy	**I-MOe** E.174. "Sinfonia . . ."
	Copyist Schmutzer
	Watermark double chain lines
Literature	Brown/CHAMBER p. 226

I: E3   STRINGS

Catalog Entry	Waldburg-Zeil f. 54

I: E4   STRINGS, 2 OBOES AND 2 HORNS

Catalog Entries	Göttweig p. 892, no. 15 Quartbuch II, p. 49, no. 17
Copies	**CS-Pnm** (Doksy) XXXIV-B-149. "Sinfonia . . ." *Copyist* local? *Watermark* Crescent with crook / six-pointed star within six-pointed (?) star **I-Fc** (Pitti) D.V.83. "Sinfonia . . ." *Copyist* Viennese No. 7 *Watermark* Baldachin with crescent on top[68], GF[37] below / ornament with 3 six-pointed stars inside (broken)[164]
Conflicting Attribution	J. C. Bach. **A-M** IV/7 (lost; Melk catalog has date 1782)
Remarks	The homogeneous material of each of the three movements does not in any way suggest J. C. Bach as a possible author.

I: F1   STRINGS, 2 OBOES AND 2 HORNS

Allegro molto

Andante

con sord.   *sempre p*

Finale

| *Copies* | **CS-Pnm** (Osek) XXXII-A-557 (title page lost) |
| | *Copyist* local? |

I-Gi(l) (Assereto?) SS.A.2.12.(H.7). "Sinfonia . . ."
Copyists Group B
Watermark Bird[62] / ℭℭ[26]

I-MOe D.291. "Sinfonia . . ."
Copyists Group A

I: F2   STRINGS (WITH 2 VIOLAS), 2 OBOES AND 2 HORNS

Vivace

Adagio cantabile

con sord.

Vivace

Catalog Entries   Göttweig p. 892, no. 16; dated 1769 P. Odo
Osek   O No. 26
Quartbuch II, p. 53, no. 30

Copies   **CS-Pnm** (Doksy) XXXIV-B-182. "Sinfonia . . ."
Copyists Group A
Watermark 3 crescents / anchor[53], W[30] below

D-ddr-Rul (Rudolstadt Hofkapell) 08. "Sinfonia . . ."
Copyist Viennese?

I-MOe D.290. "Sinfonia . . ."
Copyists Group A
Watermark 3 crescents, decreasing size[32], M(?-broken)[18] below / AS[24]

I: F3   STRINGS (WITH CELLO), 2 OBOES AND 2 HORNS

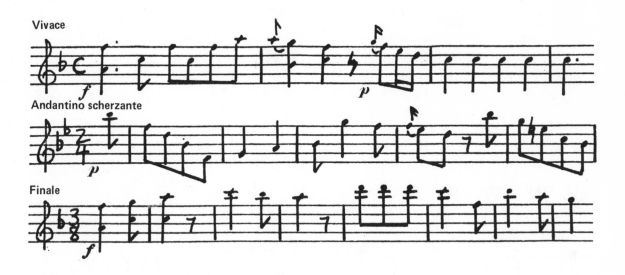

Copy   **I-MOe** E.169. "Sinfonia . . ."
              Copyist Schmutzer
              Watermark double chain lines

Literature Brown/CHAMBER p. 226

I: F4   STRINGS (WITH CELLO), 2 FLUTES (IN ANDANTINO), 2 OBOES, 2 BASSOONS AND 2 HORNS

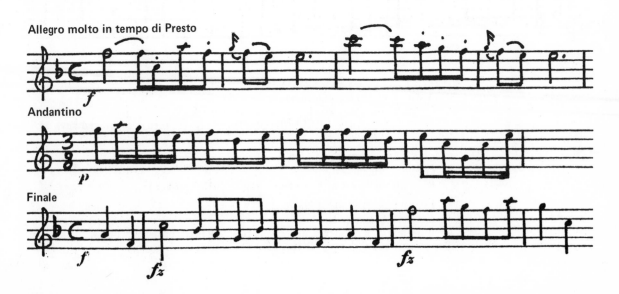

Catalog Entries	Clam-Gallas Sinfonia, Ordenetz No. 3
	Göttweig p. 893, no. 18; dated 1780 P. Marianus
	Osek O No. 25
	Quartbuch II, p. 53, no. 29
Copies	**A-GÖ** "Sinfonia . . ." Performed 5 September 1780 and 11 August 1783
	Copyist P. Marianus

A-LA   72. "Sinfonia . . ."
Copyist   local?
Watermark   Coat of arms(broken)[96] with ?R? (JRP?-broken) below

CS-Pnm (Clam-Gallas)   XLII-A-72. "Sinfonia . . ."
Copyist   local?
Watermark   3 crescents, decreasing size / primitive flower with $\frac{CG}{C}$ (?) below

I-MOe   D.288. "Sinfonia . . ."
Copyists   Group A
Watermark   Primitive flower with $\frac{CS}{C}$ (?) below

I: F5   STRINGS (WITH CELLO), 2 OBOES AND 2 HORNS

Allegro moderato

Andante

Finale

Copies	**A-Wn** S.m.3714. "Sinfonia . . ."
	Copyist Viennese No. 4
	Watermarks Eagle, I HELLER(?); Fleur de lys(broken)[53]; Crossed keys or
	crossed swords[75]

CS-K   45.c. "Sinfonia . . ."
Copyist   Viennese?
Watermark   Eagle with crown on top[112] / IHE(broken)[22]

I-Fc (Pitti)   D.V.83. "Sinfonia . . ."
Copyist   Viennese No.7
Watermark   3 crescents, decreasing size[35], REAL(broken)[26] below / baldachin
(broken)[43] with GF(broken)[33] below

I: F6   STRINGS, 2 OBOES AND 2 HORNS

Allegro molto

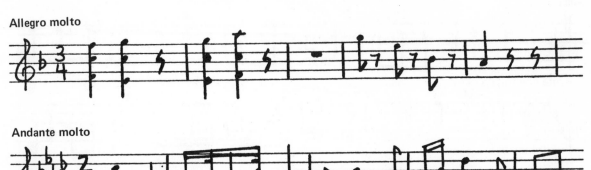

Andante molto

Menuetto moderato

Finale: Presto

Catalog Entry	Regensburg Ordonez No. 2
Copies	**CS-K** 45.e. "Sinfonia . . ."

Copyist Viennese?
Watermark 3 crescents, decreasing size / ornament with crown(?) on top[128] and W[24] inside (broken)

CS-Pnm (Doksy) XXXIV-B-174. "Sinfonia . . ."
Copyists Group A
Watermark Eagle(broken)[80] / IGS[14]

D-brd-Rtt Ordonez No. 2. "Sinfonia . . ."
Copyist Viennese No. 6?
Watermark Crescent / six-pointed star(?) star with circle inside

I-MOe D.296. "Sinfonia . . ."
Copyists Group A
Watermark 3 crescents, decreasing size[32], M (?-broken)[18] below / AS[24]

I: F7 STRINGS

Allegro

Andante non troppo Lento

Presto

Catalog Entry	Göttweig p. 892, no. 13; dated 1764 P. Leandri
Copy	**A-GÖ** "Sinfonia . . ." *Copyist* P. Leandri

I: F8 STRINGS a 3

Andante

Fuga

Menuet

Trio

Copy	**CS-Pnm** (Doksy) XXXIV-B-138. "Sinfonia . . ." *Copyists* Group A *Watermark* Heart with arrow pointing upward on top and ?B within (broken)[92]
Literature	Brown/CHAMBER p. 235 Brown/INTRODUCTION

I: F9 STRINGS

Catalog Entry	Rajhrad p. 166, no. 60
Copies	**CS-Bm** (Rajhrad) 12.850. "Sinfonia . . ." *Copyist* local? *Watermark* 3 crescents (middle one broken), REAL(?) below
	CS-Mms (Oponice) 13. "Sinfonia . . ." *Copyist* local? *Watermark* 3 crescents, decreasing size / crown
	CS-Pnm (Doksy) XXXIV-B-148. "Sinfonia . . ." *Copyist* Viennese? *Watermark* Small jumping stag[66]
Conflicting Attributions	Joseph Haydn. See Hob. I: F7 and III: F4; Landon/SYMPHONIES, p. 816, no. 97; Fuchs catalog, p. 58, no. 7; and Breitkopf catalog for 1765, col. 140

	Ignaz Holzbauer. See Landon/SYMPHONIES, p. 816, no. 97; DTB, vol. 4, p. xlv,
	    F major No. 4; Sinfonie Periodique No. 7 published by Chevardière;
	    and Johansson/FRENCH, facs. 45 (dated 1760)

	Franz Anton Schubert. See Landon/SYMPHONIES, p. 816, no. 97
Literature	Brown/CHAMBER p. 232 Brown/INTRODUCTION

I: F10   STRINGS, 2 OBOES AND 2 HORNS

Catalog Entry	Pirnitz p. 100
Conflicting Attributions	Franz Xavier Körzl. Göttweig catalog, p. 881 (with 2 oboes and 2 horns); **C-Pnm**-Doksy XXXIV-E-158
	Johann Georg Lang. **A-ST** MI 18 (with 2 horns)
Remarks	While the sources seem to point towards Körzl as the composer, the style indicates Ordonez.

I: F11   STRINGS, 2 OBOES AND 2 HORNS

Catalog Entry	Lambach p. 304
Copies	**A-LA** 71. "Sinfonia . . ."

Copyist local?
Watermark Lion(?) on hind legs[109], forelegs on oval with $_A^F{}_W^{20}{}_{18}$ inside (broken)

CS-Pnm (Doksy) XXXIV-B-151. "Sinfonia . . ."
Copyists Group A
Watermark Eagle (broken) / BVT[19] inside rectangular frame[24] (?-broken)[64]

I: F12 STRINGS

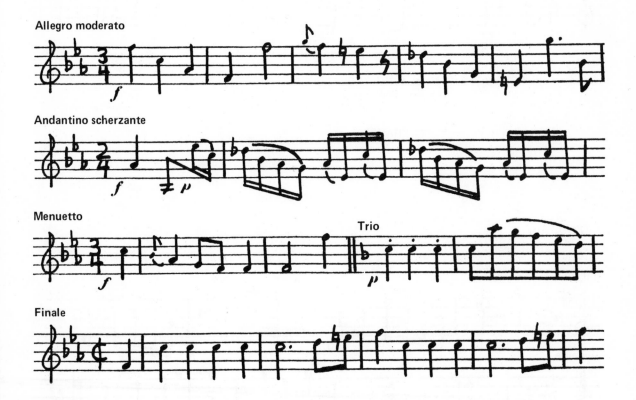

Catalog Entries	Quartbuch II, p. 28, no. 30
	Rajhrad p. 166, no. 158
Copies	**CS-Bm** (Rajhrad) A.12.851. "Sinfonia . . ."

Copyist local?
Watermark Fleur de lys (broken)[65] / CF (broken)[29]

I-MOe D.286. "Sinfonia . . ."
Copyists Group A
Watermark 2 human figures facing each other, plant in middle (?-broken),
  ALLEMODEPAPEIR (?) below (broken)

I: G1 STRINGS (WITH CELLO), 2 OBOES AND 2 HORNS

Allegro maestoso

Andante

Rondo in tempo comodo

a mezza voce

Copy	**I-MOe** E.171. "Sinfonia . . ."
	Copyist Schmutzer
	Watermark double chain lines
Literature	Brown/CHAMBER p. 226

I: G2 STRINGS

Allegro

Andante

Copy	**CS-Pnm** (Doksy) XXXIV-B-143. "Sinfonia . . ."
	Copyists Group A
	Watermark Eagle (broken) / BVT[19] inside rectangular frame[24] (?-broken)[64]

I: G3 STRINGS, 2 OBOES AND 2 HORNS

Catalog Entry	Quartbuch II, p. 55, no. 17
Copy	**CS-Pnm** (Doksy) XXXIV-B-180. "Sinfonia . . ."
	Copyists Group A
	Watermark 3 crescents / anchor[53] , W[30] below
Conflicting Attribution	Johann Vanhal. **CS-Pnm** XXXII-A-81

I: G4 STRINGS, 2 OBOES AND 2 HORNS

Catalog Entry	Breitkopf 1769, col. 339
Copies	**CS-Pnm** (Pachta) XXII-E-11. "Sinfonia . . ."
	Copyists Group A
	Watermark Eagle (broken) / IGS
	I-MOe D.283. "Sinfonia . . ."
	Copyists Group A
	Watermark Angel (holding scales in left hand?)[92] , OM at feet, RP (?)[15] below (broken)

I: G5 STRINGS, 2 OBOES AND 2 HORNS

Allegro molto

Andante

sempre p

Rondeau: Allegro

Catalog Entry	Quartbuch II, p. 55, no. 16
Copies	**I-Gi(l)** (Assereto?) SS.A.2.12.(H.7). "Sinfonia . . ."
	Copyists Group B
	Watermark Bird[62] / ƆC[23]
	I-MOe D.282. "Sinfonia . . ."
	Copyists Group A
	Watermark 2 human figures facing each other, plant in middle (?-broken),
	ALLEMODEPAPEIR(?) below (broken)

I: G6 STRINGS AND 2 OBOES

[Allegro]

Catalog Entries	Breitkopf 1766, col. 216
	Quartbuch II, p. 55, no. 19

I: G7   STRINGS (WITH CELLO), 2 OBOES AND 2 HORNS

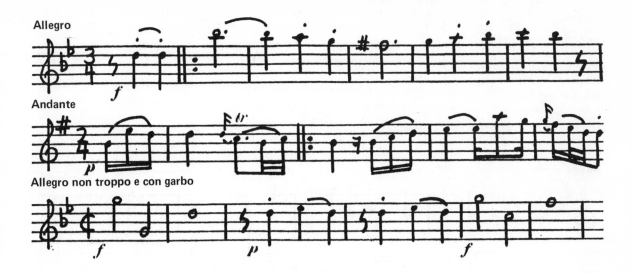

Copies	**A-Wn** S.m.3715. "Sinfonia . . ."
	Copyist Viennese No. 4
	Watermarks Eagle, I HELLER (?); Fleur de lys (broken)[53]
	CS-K 45.d. "Sinfonia . . ."
	Copyist Viennese?
	Watermark Eagle with crown on top[112] / IHE (broken)[22]
	I-Fc (Pitti) D.V.83. "Sinfonia . . ."
	Copyist Viennese No. 7
	Watermark 3 crescents, decreasing size[35], REAL (broken)[26] below / baldachin (broken)[43] with GF (broken)[33] below
Literature	Brown/CHAMBER p. 260
	Brown/INTRODUCTION

I: G8   STRINGS (WITH 2 VIOLAS) AND 2 OBOES

Catalog Entry   Quartbuch II, p. 55, no. 18

Copy   **I-MOe** D.295. "Sinfonia . . ."
Copyists Group A
Watermark 3 crescents, decreasing size[32], M (?-broken)[18] below / AS[24]

I: A1   STRINGS, 2 OBOES AND 2 HORNS

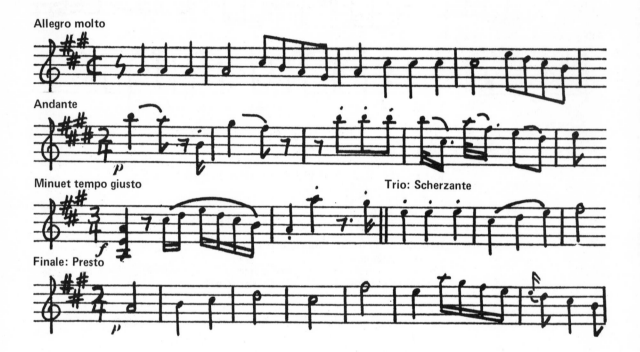

Allegro molto

Andante

Minuet tempo giusto   **Trio: Scherzante**

Finale: Presto

Catalog Entry   Göttweig p. 891, no. 9; dated 1764 P. Leandri

Copies   **B-Bc** W.7779. "Sinfonia . . ."
Watermarks Simple crown[23] with GR[15] below; Circular coat of arms with
double border, crown on top, letters N (?) ?YHE? (broken) inside,
B_UB (broken) on border[134]

CS-Pnm (Doksy) XXXIV-B-175. "Sinfonia . . ."
Copyist Viennese?
Watermark Eagle (broken)[80] / IGS[14]

CS-Pnm (Osek) XXXII-A-344. "Sinfonia . . ."
Copyists Group A
Watermark 2 human figures[86] facing each other, plant[41] in middle (?-broken),
ALLEMODEPAPEIR (?) below (broken)

CS-Pnm (Pachta) XXII-E-5. "Sinfonia . . ."
Copyists Group A
Watermark Eagle (broken) / IGS

Literature   Landon/HAYDN p. 9

I: A2   STRINGS, 2 OBOES AND 2 HORNS

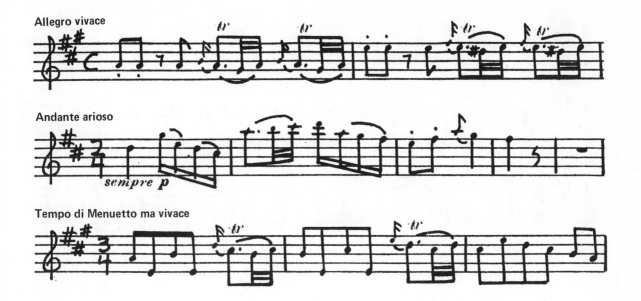

Copy	**I-MOe** E.173. "Sinfonia . . ."
	Copyist Schmutzer
	Watermark double chain lines
Literature	Brown/CHAMBER p. 226
	Landon/PROBLEMS p. 35

I: A3

[Allegro]

Catalog Entry	Klosterneuburg p. 84

I: A4   STRINGS, 2 OBOES AND 2 HORNS

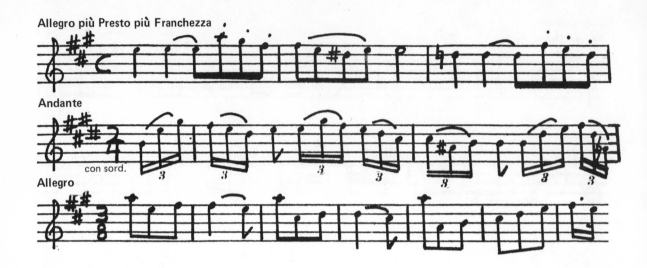

Catalog Entry	Quartbuch II, p. 36, no. 13
Copy	**I-MOe** D.281. "Sinfonia . . ."
	Copyists Group A
	Watermark 2 human figures facing each other, plant in middle (?-broken), ALLEMODEPAPEIR (?) below (broken)

I: A5   STRINGS a 3

Copy	**CS-Pnm** (Doksy) XXXIV-B-139. "Sinfonia . . ."
	Copyists Group A
	Watermark Eagle (broken)[80] / IGS[14]
Literature	Brown/CHAMBER p. 235

I: A6   STRINGS, 2 OBOES AND 2 HORNS

Allegro molto

Grazioso

Presto

Catalog Entries	Breitkopf 1766, col. 216
	Göttweig p. 892, no. 12; dated 1764 P. Leandri

Copies   **A-GÖ**   "Sinfonia . . ."
Copyist   local
Watermark   Coat of arms with crown on top (broken)[115] / ornament[75] with
    F (?)CP[16] below (broken)

CS-KRm   IV.A.232.   "Sinfonia . . ."
Copyists   Group A
Watermark   2 human figures facing each other, plant in middle (?-broken),
    ALLEMODEPAPEIR (?) below (broken)

CS-Pnm   (Pachta)   XXII-E-6.   "Sinfonia . . ."
Copyists   Group A
Watermark   ADLER (?)[30], IPR (?)[32] below, indecipherable object above (broken)

I-Gi(l)   (Assereto?)   SS.A.2.12.(H.7).   "Sinfonia . . ."
Copyists   Group B
Watermark   Bird[62] / ⊃C[23]

I-MOe   D.293.   "Sinfonia . . ."
Copyists   Group A

I: A7   STRINGS AND SOLO VIOLIN

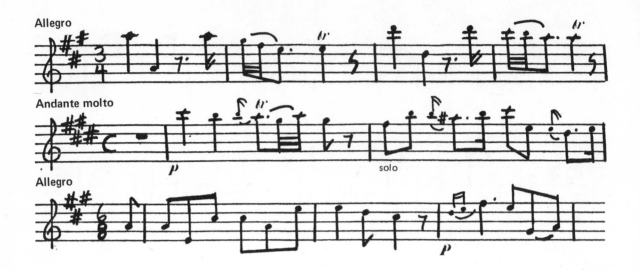

Catalog Entry	Göttweig p. 890, no. 3; dated 1759 P. Leandri
Copies	**A-SCH** (lost)
	CS-Pnm (Doksy) XXXIV-B-142. "Sinfonia . . ."
	Copyists Group A
	Watermark Eagle (broken) / BVT[19] inside rectangular frame[24] (?-broken)[64]

I: A8   STRINGS, 2 OBOES AND 2 HORNS

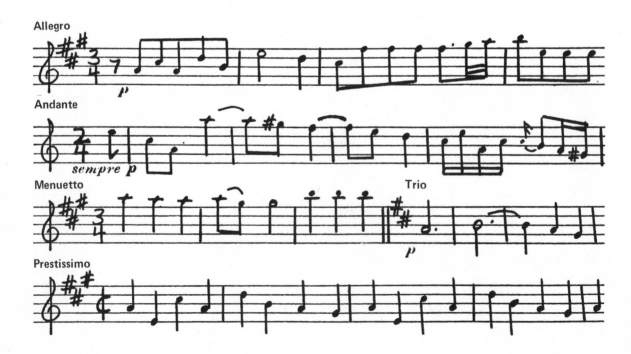

Catalog Entries	Donau Sigmaringen Ordonez No. 3 ("Symphonia")

Copies	**CS-Pnm** (Pachta) XXII-E-13. "Sinfonia . . ."
	Copyists Group A
	Watermarks 2 human figures facing each other, plant in middle (?-broken),
	   ALLEMODEPAPEIR (?) below (broken); Crescent with crook / star
	   with circle inside
	
	D-brd-DO (Stift Villingen) Mus.ms.1482. "Symphonia . . . 1772"
	   (without oboes and horns)
	Copyist Francisci Caroli Stuckler
	Watermark Coat of arms with crown on top, bell with visible clapper below,
	   fleur de lys inside

Conflicting Attribution	Joseph Haydn. See Hob. I: A6; Göttweig catalog, p. 864, no. 38 (dated 1766
	   P. Leandri); Quartbuch, II, p. 35, no. 3; and **A-Wgm** XI/40926 ("Parthia"),
	   score by Pohl from lost Göttweig parts

Literature	Landon/PROBLEMS p. 35 Landon/SYMPHONIES pp. 25-26; p. 820, no. 119; Supplement, pp. 29, 58 Larsen/DHK p. 123 (III: A2) Larsen/QUARTBUCH p. 121

I: A9   STRINGS a 3

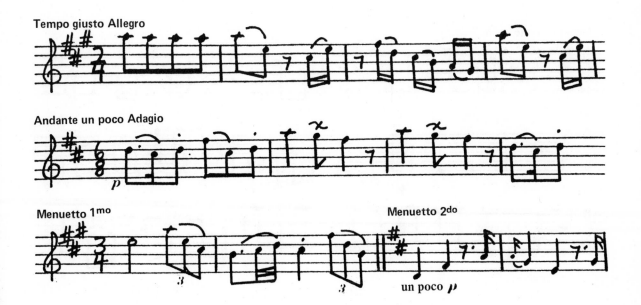

Copy	**H-KE** (Festetics) KO/46. "Sinfonia . . ." *Copyist* Viennese *Watermark* Eagle (broken)[72] / IGS[16]

66 / Group I

I: A10 STRINGS

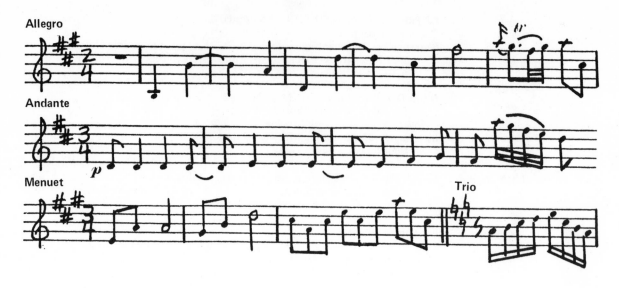

> *Copy* **CS-Pnm** (Doksy) XXXIV-B-141. "Sinfonia . . ."
> *Copyists* Group A
> *Watermark* Eagle (broken) / BVT[19] inside rectangular frame[24] (?-broken)[64]

I: A11 STRINGS

> *Copies* **CS-Pnm** (Doksy) XXXIV-B-147. "Sinfonia . . ."
> *Copyists* Group A
> *Watermark* Eagle (broken)[80] / IGS[14]
>
> **D-brd-MÜu** (Rheda) Ms.564. "Sinfonia . . ."
> *Copyist* local?

I: B♭1

Copies **CS-Bm** (St. Brno) A.19.603. "Symphonia ..."
Copyist local

CS-Pnm (Doksy) XXXIV-B-140. "Sinfonia ..."
Copyists Group A
Watermark Eagle (broken)[80] / IGS[14]

I: B♭2 STRINGS (WITH 2 VIOLAS), 2 OBOES AND 2 HORNS

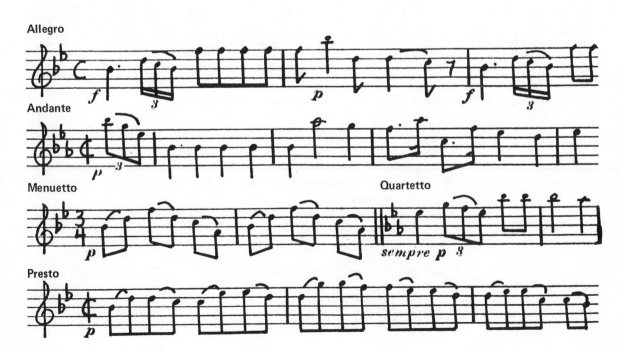

Catalog Entry	Göttweig p. 890, no. 4; copied by P. Odo
Copies	**CS-Pnm** (Doksy) XXXIV-B-179. "Sinfonia . . ."

Copyists Group A
Watermark 3 crescents, decreasing size[32] / primitive flower[17] with $\frac{CS23}{C\,(?)\,18}$ below

I-MOe D.297. "Sinfonia . . ."
Copyists Group A

I: B♭3 STRINGS

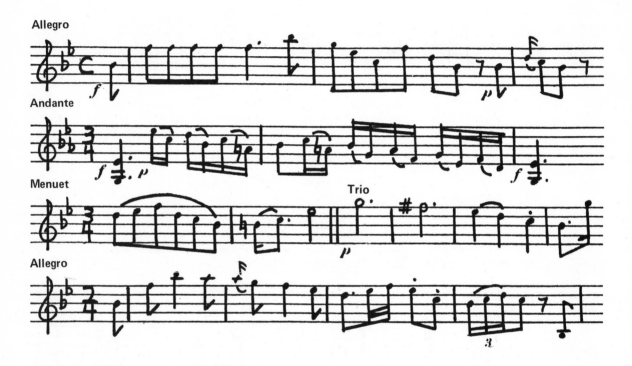

Catalog Entry	Göttweig p. 892, no. 14; dated 1765 P. Leandri
Copies	**A-GÖ** "Parthia . . ." (with 2 horns)

Copyist P. Leandri
Watermark Coat of arms with crown on top (broken)[115] / ornament[75] with
F(?)CP[16] below (broken)

A-M VI/2882 (formerly of the collection of **A-Wgm**). "Sinfonia . . ."
Copyist Viennese No. 1
Watermark 3 crescents, decreasing size, M[21] below (off center) / crown with
cross[18] above (broken)

I-MOe D.285. "Sinfonia . . ."
Copyists Group A
Watermark Angel (holding scales in left hand?)[92], OM at feet, RP (?)[15]
below (broken)

Literature	Brown/CHAMBER p. 237
	Wellesz-Sternfeld/SYMPHONY p. 401

I: B♭4   STRINGS (WITH 2 VIOLAS AND CELLO), 2 OBOES AND 2 HORNS

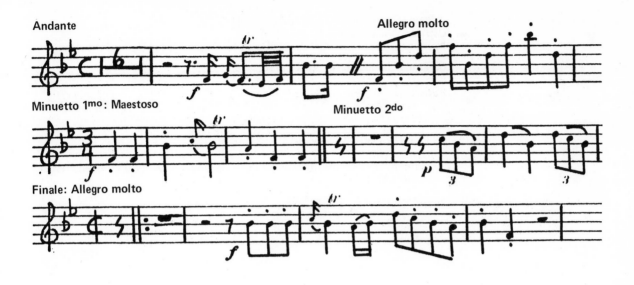

Copies   **A-Wn**   S.m.3716.   "Sinfonia . . ."
Copyist   Viennese No. 4
Watermark   Crossed keys or crossed swords[75]; Fleur de lys (broken)[53]

CS-Bm (Rajhrad)   A.12.852.   "Sinfonia . . . Procuravit P. Maurus: Reg: Chori 779"
Copyist   P. Maurus
Watermark   Fleur de lys[62] / ℂ(?)[43]

I-Fc (Pitti)   D.V.83.   "Sinfonia . . ."
Copyist   Viennese No. 7
Watermark   3 crescents, decreasing size[35], REAL (broken)[26] below / baldachin (broken)[43] with GF (broken)[33] below

I: B♭5   STRINGS, 2 OBOES AND 2 HORNS

Catalog Entries	Osek O No. 27
	Quartbuch II, p. 37, no. 8

Copies	**A-Wgm** (Carrara) XIII/6377. "Sinfonia . . ."

Copyist   Viennese No. 4
Watermark   Bird[50] / ƆC[23] / wheel with baldachin on top[60], AFC[34] below

CS-Pnm (Clam-Gallas) XLII-C-336. "Sinfonia . . ."
Copyist   Viennese
Watermark   3 crescents, decreasing size[46], C[20] below (off center) / thin (?) ornament[101] on chain line with F (?) on lower left, C (?)[39] on lower right (broken)

CS-Pnm (Doksy) XXXIV-B-152. "Sinfonia . . ."
Copyist   Viennese No. 4?
Watermark   3 crescents, decreasing size / six-pointed (?) star / crooked crescent / IF (?-broken)[25]

Literature	Brown/CHAMBER p. 225

I: B♭6   STRINGS (WITH 2 VIOLAS)

Catalog Entry	Göttweig p. 891, no. 10; dated 1764 P. Leandri

Copies	**A-GÖ** "Sinfonia . . ."

Copyist   P. Leandri
Watermark   Coat of arms with crown on top (broken)[115] / ornament[75] with F(?)CP[16] below (broken)

D-brd-HR   III, 4 ½, 4o, 566. "Sinfonia . . ."
Copyist   Viennese?
Watermark   4 with anchor bottom, ASF (?) below / ML / $ B

I-MOe   D.294. "Sinfonia . . ."
Copyists   Group A

Conflicting Attribution	Dittersdorf. **A-Ssp** (lost)

Literature	LaRue/MGG col. 1812

I: B♭7 STRINGS AND 2 OBOES

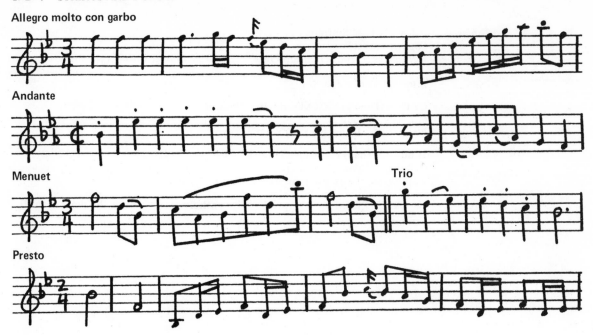

Allegro molto con garbo

Andante

Menuet   Trio

Presto

Catalog Entries	Quartbuch II, p. 37, no. 9
	Sigmaringen Ordonez No. 5
Copies	**CS-Bm** (Pirnitz) A.9418 (title page only). "Sinfonia . . ."
	CS-Pnm (Osek) XXXII-A-399. "Serenade . . ."
	Copyist local
Conflicting Attribution	Vanhal. Quartbuch I, p. 9, no. 52

I: B♭8 STRINGS

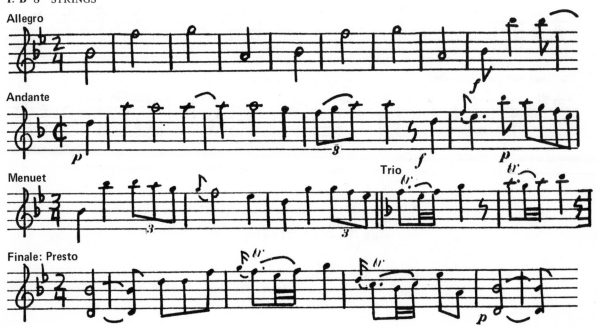

Allegro

Andante

Menuet   Trio

Finale: Presto

Catalog Entries	Hummel p. 50
	Lambach p. 304

Copies   **A-LA**   161.   "Sinfonia . . ."
Copyist   local?
Watermark   Lion (?) on hind legs[109], forelegs on oval with $^{F20}_{A}W18$ inside (broken)

B-Bc   W.7779.   "Sinfonia . . ."   (with 2 oboes and 2 horns)

CS-Pnm (Doksy)   XXXIV-B-146.   "Sinfonia . . ."
Copyists   Group A
Watermark   Eagle (broken)[80] / IGS[14]

H-Bn (Esterházy)   Ms.mus.IV.601.   "Parthia . . . Ex rebus Franciscei Nigst"
Copyists   Viennese? and Nigst
Watermark   Large jumping stag (broken)[134] / IGS[22]

Literature   Harich/ESTERHÁZY   VII, p. 45   [Not entirely clear if this is the work identified.]

I: B1   STRINGS (WITH CELLO), 2 OBOES AND 2 HORNS

Copies   **A-Wn**   S.m.3717.   "Sinfonia . . ."
Copyist   Viennese No. 4
Watermark   Eagle, I HELLER (?)

I-Fc (Pitti)   D.V.83.   "Sinfonia . . ."
Copyist   Viennese No. 7
Watermark   3 crescents, decreasing size[35], REAL (broken)[26] below / baldachin
(broken)[43] with GF (broken)[33] below

I/*Q*: C1   STRINGS, 2 CLARINI AND TIMPANI

Allegro molto

Andante

Presto

Catalog Entry	Lambach p. 304
Copies	**A-KR** H27/200. "Sinfonia . . . Sparry 1757" *Copyist* Franz Sparry
	A-LA 67. "Sinfonia . . . Joanne Carlo Ordonez" *Copyist* local?
Conflicting Attribution	Georg Christoph Wagenseil. **A-GÖ** with date 1759 and the following finale in place of the Presto:

Allegro

Literature	Kucaba/WAGENSEIL II, p. 14 Scholz-Michelitsch/WAGENSEIL p. 100, no. 356

I/*Q*: C2   STRINGS

Allegro

Andante

Tempo di Menuetto

Copy	**CS-Pnm** (Doksy) XXXIV-B-177. "Sinfonia . . ."
	Copyists Group A
	Watermark Eagle (broken)[80] / IGS[14]
Conflicting Attribution	Georg Christoph Wagenseil. Lambach catalog, p. 325 (music lost)
Literature	Kucaba/WAGENSEIL II, p. 24
Remarks	Not in Scholz-Michelitsch/WAGENSEIL

I/*S*: C1   STRINGS, 2 OBOES, BASSOON AND 2 CLARINI

Allegro vivace

Andante grazioso

[Presto]

Catalog Entry	Göttweig p. 891, no. 8
Probable Author	Nicola Piccini. See Breitkopf catalog for 1770, col. 379; Clam-Gallas catalog, P No. 3; Quartbuch, II, p. 42, no. 46; **D-ddr-Bds**-Königliche Hausbibliothek 3417 and numerous other copies.

I/S: C2 STRINGS

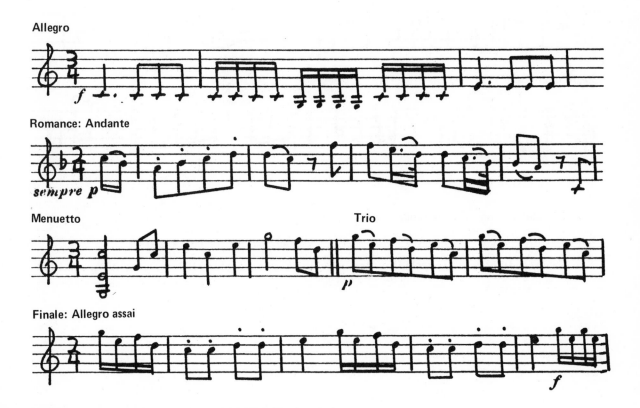

Copy	**A-Wn** S.m.12170 (title page lost)
	Copyist Viennese
	Watermark 3 crescents, decreasing size / primitive flower with $\frac{CS}{C}$ below
Literature	Brown/CHAMBER p. 224
Remarks	The only evidence for the authorship of Ordonez is the catalog of **A-Wn**. Stylistic observations do not corroborate this citation.

I/*S*: D1   STRINGS, 2 OBOES AND 2 HORNS

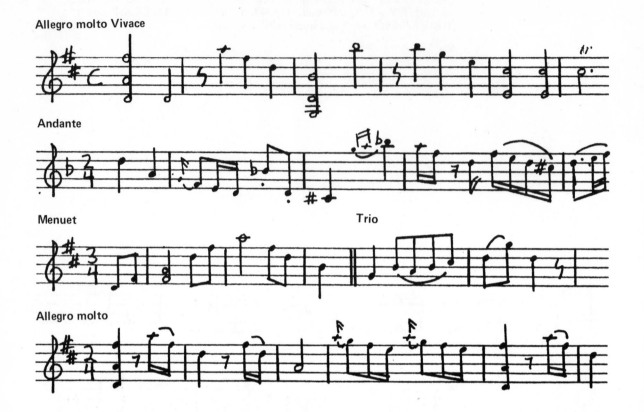

Catalog Entry	Breitkopf 1767, col. 262
Conflicting Attributions	Leopold Hofmann, Padre Martini, Georg Christoph Wagenseil
Probable Author	Leopold Hofmann. See Breitkopf catalog for 1773, col. 483; **A-Wn** S.m.1800 and numerous other copies.

Group II
OTHER WORKS
FOR ORCHESTRA

IIa: D1   CONCERTO FOR VIOLIN, STRINGS, 2 OBOES AND 2 HORNS

Copy	**A-Wn** S.m.11090. "Concerto . . ."
	Copyist Viennese No. 4
	Watermark Crossed keys or crossed swords[75]
Literature	Hanslick/VIRTUOSENCONCERTE p. 255

IIb: 1   SERENADE FOR THE FIREWORKS DISPLAY "DAS DENKMAL DES FRIEDENS" FOR 31 WIND INSTRUMENTS IN TWO CHOIRS

Literature	Brown/INTRODUCTION
	Pohl/HAYDN II, p. 152
	PZ 1779, no. 53
	WD 1779, Anhang zum no. 49

IIb: 2 PARTITA FOR STRINGS, 2 OBOES, BASSOON, 2 HORNS, 2 CLARINI, TIMPANI, SNARE DRUM AND CYMBALS

Catalog Entry   Traeg p. 114, no. 150 ("Parttita Turca per la caccia")

IIc: 1 MINUETS FOR 2 VIOLINS AND BASS

Copy   **A-Wgm**   XV/2834.   "Menuetti"
           Copyist   Viennese
           Watermark   Heart with crown on top and six-pointed star within (broken)[76] /
                    IG (?) S[23]

Remarks   Probably an arrangement of a fuller orchestration.

IIc: 2   BALLET FOR STRINGS (WITH 2 VIOLAS), 2 FLUTES, 2 OBOES, 2 BASSOONS AND 2 HORNS

ACT I

Un poco Andante

Chaconne: Allegro non troppo

Andante

Allegro

Andante grazioso

Menuetto

Allegretto

Allegro

Un poco Andante

Allegro non troppo

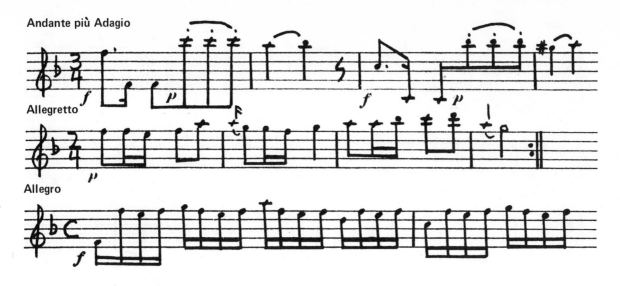

ACT II

Allegretto

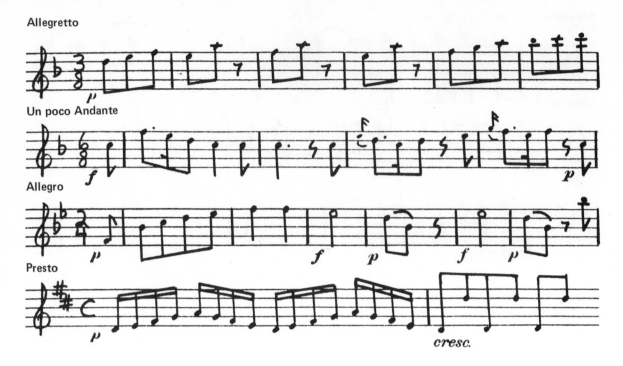

Un poco Andante

Allegro

Presto

ACT III

Andante grazioso

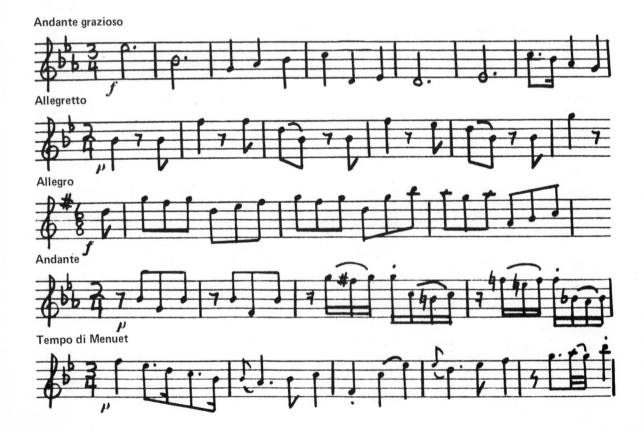

Allegretto

Allegro

Andante

Tempo di Menuet

Allegro

Andante

Finale: Tempo di Menuet

Catalog Entry	Göttweig p. 890, no. 1; dated 1758 P. Leandri
Copy	**A-GÖ** "Pantomima . . ."
	Copyist Viennese
	Watermark 3 crescents, decreasing size /ʊₚ¹⁴ with FG (broken)²⁸ below
Literature	Brown/ INTRODUCTION

Group III
DIVERTIMENTI, ETC.,
FOR 8 TO 5 PARTS

IIIa: F1   OCTET FOR 2 OBOES, 2 ENGLISH HORNS, 2 HORNS AND 2 BASSOONS

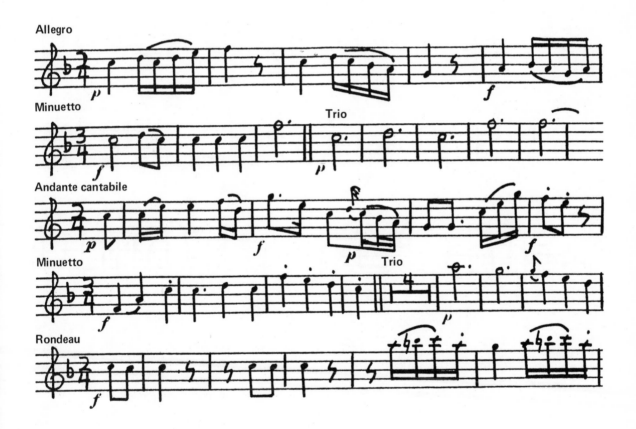

Copy   **CS-K**   26a   (English horn I part lost).   "Notturno . . ."
Copyist   Viennese?
Watermark   Eagle with heart inside (broken)[72]/ I HELLER (?) [double chain lines]

Literature   Brown/INTRODUCTION

IIIb: F1   SEXTET FOR STRINGS a 4 AND 2 HORNS

Catalog Entry	Sigmaringen Ordonez No. 2 ("Concertino . . .")
Copy	**D-brd-HR** III, 4 ½, 2°, 1072. "Cassatio . . ." *Copyist* local? *Watermark* Coat of arms with crown on top, post horn in middle (?) / primitive flower
Conflicting Attribution	Joseph Haydn. See Hob. II: F6 and Breitkopf catalog for 1768, col. 307
Literature	Brown/CHAMBER pp. 228, 231-32, 235, 249 Brown/INTRODUCTION Landon/MGG col. 194 Landon/PROBLEMS p. 36 Larsen/DHK p. 123 (III: F12)

IIIc: E♭1   QUINTET FOR VIOLIN, VIOLA, BASS AND 2 HORNS

Allegretto

Catalog Entry	Pirnitz 100c ("Cassatio con corni . . . lma")
Conflicting Attribution	Joseph Haydn. See Hob. II: E♭9 and Sigmaringen catalog, no. 60
Literature	Brown/CHAMBER pp. 227, 231-32, 259
	Brown/INTRODUCTION

IIIc: E♭2   QUINTET FOR 2 VIOLINS, 2 VIOLAS AND BASS

Allegro

Menuetto   **Trio**

Adagio

Menuetto   **Trio**

Finale: Allegro

Copy	**A-Wn** (Kaisersammlung) S.m.11481. "Divertimento . . ." *Copyist* N. H., dated 1790
Literature	Brown/CHAMBER pp. 224, 239, 241, 249 Brown/INTRODUCTION

IIIc: F1 QUINTET FOR VIOLIN, VIOLA, BASS AND 2 HORNS

Vivace

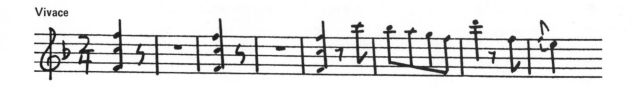

Menuetto   **Trio**

Andante

Finale

Conflicting Attribution	Joseph Haydn. See Hob. II: F4; Breitkopf catalog for 1768, col. 306; Fuchs catalog, p. 31, no. 3; Sigmaringen catalog, "Haydn," no. 58; **A-Wgm** XI/40929 ("Quintetto . . ."; score by Pohl based on Jahn); **B-Bc** nineteenth-century score [information from G. Feder]
Literature	Brown/CHAMBER pp. 228, 231-32, 238, 259 Brown/INTRODUCTION Larsen/DHK p. 123 (III: F11)
Remarks	Stylistic as well as bibliographic parallels with IIIc: E♭1 and F2 suggest Ordonez is the correct author.

IIIc: F2   QUINTET FOR VIOLIN, VIOLA, BASS AND 2 HORNS

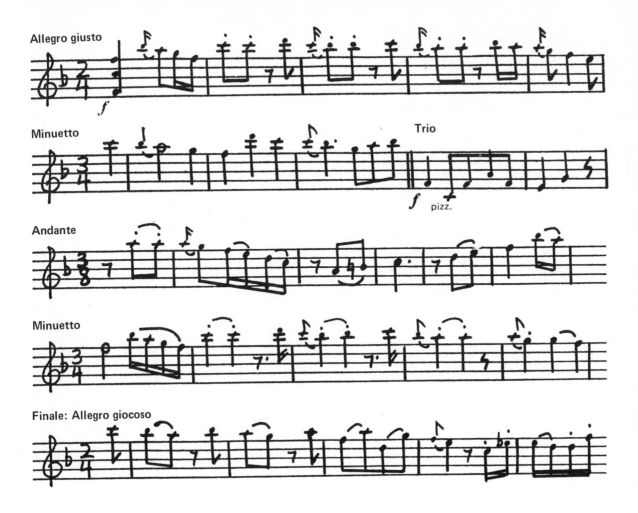

Catalog Entries	Breitkopf 1768, col. 306
	Göttweig p. 892, no. 11; dated 1763 P. Leandri
	Pirnitz 100c ("Cassatio con corni . . . 2da")
Copy	**A-GÖ** "Notturno . . ."
	Copyist P. Leandri
	Watermark Heart with crown on top and six-pointed star within (?-broken)[77] / IGS (broken)[20]
Conflicting Attribution	Joseph Haydn. See Hob. II: F5 and Fuchs catalog, p. 31, no. 2
Literature	Brown/CHAMBER pp. 225, 227, 231-32, 235, 238, 259
	Brown/INTRODUCTION
	Landon/MGG col. 194
	Landon/OPERA 1 AND 2 p. 186
	Landon/PROBLEMS p. 36
	Larsen/DHK p. 123 (III: F9)
	Scott/OPUS TWO AND THREE pp. 9-11

Group IV
STRING QUARTETS

STRING QUARTETS

IV: F4 and B♭3   2 VIOLINS, VIOLA AND BASS

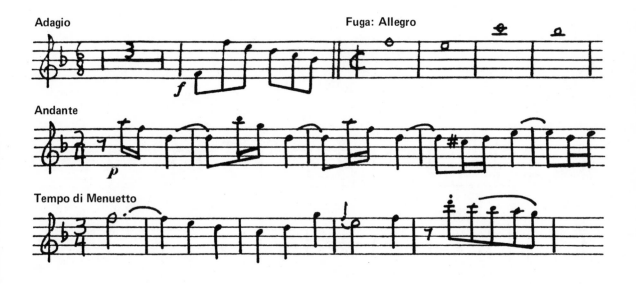

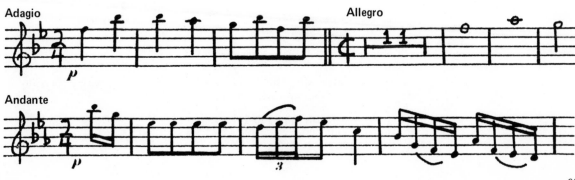

Finale: Allegro

Catalog Entry	Klosterneuburg (only B♭3) p. 80 ("Sinfonia")
Copies	**D-ddr-Bds** (Königliche Hausbibliothek) M3262, M3267. "Divertimento . . . da Camera"
	Copyist Viennese No. 6?
	Watermark Coat of arms with crown on top (broken)[186] / REINF ____ (?)[33]
	GB-Lcm (Salomons) MS733. "Quartetti . . ."
	Watermark 3 crescents, decreasing size / AM (broken)[27] / bow with arrow through it (broken)[33]
Literature	Brown/CHAMBER pp. 224, 228-29, 235-36, 240, 246-49, 258
	Brown/QUARTETS pp. 315-16, 318

IV: A4   2 VIOLINS, VIOLA AND BASS

Andante più Adagio

Allegro moderato

Allegro molto

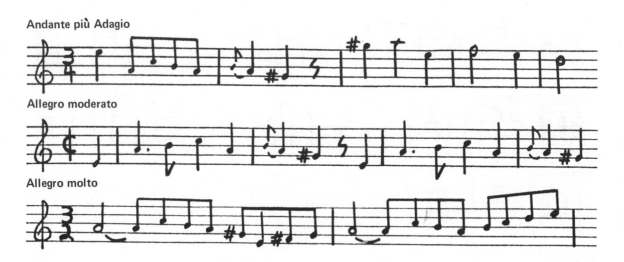

Copy	**A-Wn** S.m.12169. "Partitta a Quatro . . ."
	Copyist Viennese
	Watermark 3 crescents / thin (?) ornament[101] on chain line with F (?) on lower left, C (?)[39] on lower right (broken)
Literature	Barrett-Ayres/HAYDN pp. 320-21
	Brown/CHAMBER pp. 224, 240, 242-43, 245
	Brown/QUARTETS p. 315

IV: A1, F3, C4, E♭2, B♭1 and G1. Opus 1   2 VIOLINS, VIOLA AND BASS

Andante un poco Lento

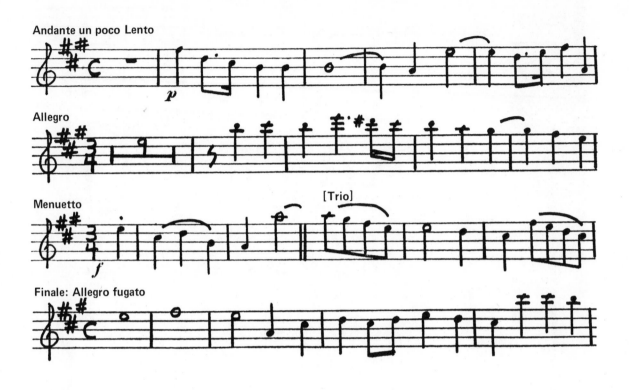

Allegro

Menuetto

[Trio]

Finale: Allegro fugato

Andante

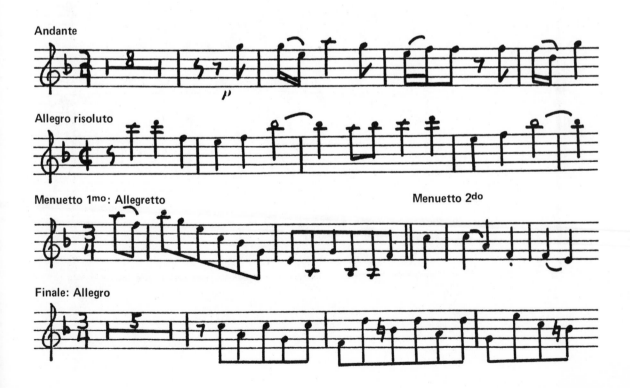

Allegro risoluto

Menuetto 1mo: Allegretto   **Menuetto 2do**

Finale: Allegro

SEI
QUARTETTI
Per due Violini, Viola e Basso
Composti
Del Signore
DE ORDONNIZ.

Prezzo 9ᵗᵗ
Opera Iᵃ

A LION

Chez Guera, Editeur et Mᵈ de Musique; Place des Terreaux :
A PARIS au Bureau du Journal de Musique rue Montmartre.
chez Mˢ les Mᵈˢ de Musique
Gravé par Charpentier fils
30

**Title page
from
Guera print of
String Quartets
Opus 1**

Andante

Allegro non troppo Presto

Menuetto 1mo: Andante   **Menuetto 2do**

Finale: Allegro

Andante

Allegro

Menuetto: Allegretto   **Trio**

Finale: Allegro molto

Catalog Entries	Clam-Gallas Quartetti, No. 25
	Náměšť
	d'Ogny p. 36
	Quartbuch I, p. 5, no. 58; p. 29, no. 52; p. 14, no. 54; p. 25, no. 81; p. 9, no. 55; p. 34, no. 66

Copies

A-GÖ (Carrara) (F3 lost) (originally in **A-Wgm**: XII 6378). "Quartetto . . ."
Copyist Viennese
Watermark 3 crescents, decreasing size[38], REAL (?-broken)[24] below / baldachin (?)[31] with GB[36] below (broken)

A-LA 169, 170. "Tre Quartetti . . ."
Copyist local?
Watermarks 3 crescents, decreasing size / bow with arrow through it (broken)[33]; Helmet[83] / 4[37], WMS[20] below; Ornament with crown on top and ^Z_CA[24]$_{23}$ inside (broken)

A-Wgm IX/8190. "Sei Quartetti . . . Opera Seconda"
Copyist Viennese (same as **H-Ke** below)
Watermarks Baldachin with GF below / ornament with 3 six-pointed stars inside and crescent on top; 3 crescents, decreasing size / ornament with crown on top and W inside (broken)

A-Wn (Kaisersammlung) S.m.12145-12150. "Quartetto . . ."
Copyists N. H., dated 1786, and Group A
Watermarks Ornament with crown on top[152] and ^Z_CA[21]$_{19}$ inside (broken); 3 crescents, decreasing size[30], REAL (broken)[17] / GFA[24]

CS-Bm (Náměšť) A16.590-16.591. "III Quartetti . . ."
Copyist Viennese No. 5
Watermark 3 crescents, decreasing size (first one crooked) / baldachin (?-broken) / VB (or AB?)

CS-K 41. "Quartetto . . ."
Copyist Viennese No. 5
Watermark Baldachin with crescent on top, GF below / ornament with 3 six-pointed stars inside (broken)

CS-Pnm (Clam-Gallas) XLII-C-318-323. "Quartetto . . ."
Copyist local?
Watermark 3 crescents, decreasing size / six-pointed star within six-pointed (?) star / crooked crescent / IF (HF?-broken)

CS-Pnm (Hradiště Choustníkovo) XIII-D-306 (only C4). "Partitta . . ."
Copyist Viennese No. 4
Watermark Eagle (broken) / IGS

GB-Lcm (Salomons) MS733. "Quartetti . . ."
Copyist local?
Watermark 3 crescents, decreasing size / AM (broken)[27] / bow with arrow through it (broken)[33]

H-Bn Ms.mus.IV.426/1-4. "VI Sonate . . ."
Copyists Group B
Watermark 3 crescents, decreasing size / ornament with crown on top and W inside (broken)

H-KE (Festetics) K 0/13. "Quartetto . . ."
Copyist Viennese (same as **A-Wgm** above)
Watermark 3 crescents, decreasing size / ornament (broken) with W[25] inside and crown on top

Print	SEI/QUARTETTI/Per due Violini, Viola e Basso/Composti/del Signore/DE ORDONNIZ/Prezzo 9^{tt}/Opera Ia/A LION/chez Guera, Editeur et Md. de Musique, Place des Terreaux./A PARIS Au Bureau du Journal de Musique rue Montmartre/chez Mrs les Mds. de Musique/Gravé par Charpentier fils/30.

Print SEI/QUARTETTI/Per due Violini, Viola e Basso/Composti/del Signore/DE ORDONNIZ/Prezzo 9^{tt}/Opera Ia/A LION/chez Guera, Editeur et Md. de Musique, Place des Terreaux./A PARIS Au Bureau du Journal de Musique rue Montmartre/chez Mrs les Mds. de Musique/Gravé par Charpentier fils/30.

Announcements   *Almanach Musical* (Paris) for 1778, p. 103; Böhme catalog for 1800, p. 25; Breitkopf catalog for 1778, col. 639; Westphal catalog for 1782, p. 32

Location **I-Nc** MS1643-1646

Modern Edition   Edited by A. Peter Brown. Madison, Wisconsin: A-R Editions, 197? (Recent Researches of the Pre-Classical, Classical and Early Romantic Eras)

Literature
Barrett-Ayres/HAYDN   pp. 319-20, 322
Brown/CHAMBER   pp. 224-30, 235, 238, 240-46, 249-50, 257-58, 260-61
Brown/INTRODUCTION
Brown/QUARTETS   p. 316
Kirkendale/FUGE   p. 156

IV: B♭2, D4, C3, A3, F5 and G4. Opus 2   2 VIOLINS, VIOLA AND BASS

Adagio

Fuga: Allegro

Menuetto 1mo   **Menuetto 2do**

Andante

Fuga

Menuetto 1mo   **Menuetto 2do**

Finale: Moderato

Catalog Entries	Clam-Gallas Quartetti, No. 22
	Quartbuch I, p. 6, no. 9 [as Vanhal]; p. 15, no. 11; p. 11, no. 10; p. 1, no. 8; p. 28, no. 32; p. 30, no. 9
Copies	**A-GÖ** (Carrara) (originally in **A-Wgm**: XII 6379). "Quartetto . . ."

Copyist Viennese
Watermark 3 crescents, decreasing size[40], REAL (?-broken)[24] below and off-center to left / ornament with W inside and crown on top (broken)[129]

A-M IV/1798 (only C3, D4, F5). "Quartetto . . ."
Copyist Viennese
Watermark 3 crescents[40], REAL (broken)[23] below / P (?)S[23]

A-Wgm IX/2042 (A3, F5, and G4 missing Violin I). "Quartetti . . .
 Opera prima"
Copyist Viennese
Watermark 3 crescents / baldachin with GF below / ornament with 3 six-pointed stars inside and crescent on top

A-Wn (Kaisersammlung) S.m.12151-12156. "Quartetto . . ."
Copyist N. H., dated 1786
Watermark 3 crescents, decreasing size[30], REAL (broken)[17] below / GFA[24]

CS-Bm (Neureisch) A17.817-17.818 (only C3 and D4). "Quartetto . . ."
Copyist Schmutzer
Watermark double chain lines

CS-Pnm (Horšovský Týn) XLIX.C.505 (only C3, D4, F5, G4). "Partitta . . ."
Copyist Viennese No. 4

D-ddr-Bds (Königliche Hausbibliothek)   M3269, M3264, M3266, M3263,
   M3265, M3268. "Divertimento . . ."
Copyist   Viennese No. 6?
Watermark   Coat of arms with crown on top (broken)[186] / REINF____(?)[33]

GB-Lbm (Zoeller)   ADD 32.396 f.46-74 (title page lost)
Copyist   Viennese?
Watermarks   Coat of arms, crown on top / AH (EISLER or HEILIG?); Eagle /
   (HELLER?)

GB-Lcm (Salomons)   MS733. "VI Quartetti . . ."
Watermark   3 crescents, decreasing size / AM (broken)[27] / bow with arrow
   through it (broken)[33]

H-KE (Festetics)   K 0/13. "Quartetto . . ."
Copyist   Viennese
Watermark   Fleur de lys (broken)[59] / (crossed keys or crossed swords?)

I-Gi(l) (Assereto?)   SS.A.1.9.(G.7). "Sei Sonate . . ."
Copyists   Group B

Literature   Barrett-Ayres/HAYDN p. 322
           Brown/CHAMBER pp. 224-30, 235, 238, 240-46, 249, 258
           Brown/QUARTETS p. 315
           Kirkendale/FUGE   pp. 100, 137, 157, 165, 171

Remarks   The print of Op. 2 by Guera of Lyon mentioned in Kirkendale/FUGE (p. 36),
           Landon/MGG (col. 194), and Landon/PROBLEMS (p. 34) apparently
           never existed.

IV: G3, D1, C2, A2, F2 and D3   2 VIOLINS, VIOLA AND BASS

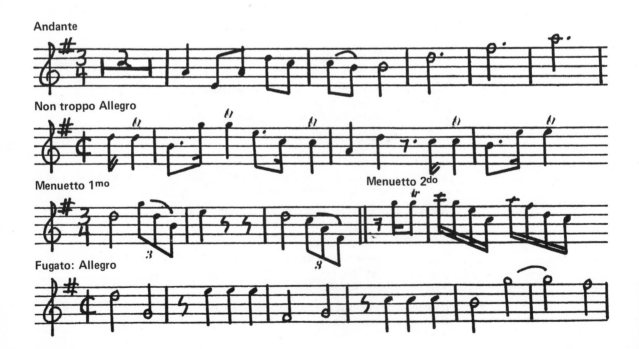

Allegro moderato

Menuetto

Trio

mezza voce

Adagio cantabile

Fugato: Allegro

Catalog Entry	Náměšť
Copies	**A-Wn** (Kaisersammlung) S.m.12157-12162. "Quartetto . . ." *Copyist* N. H., dated 1788 *Watermark* Man figure, right leg forward, holding torch (?) in right hand (broken)[116] [double chain lines]
	CS-Bm (Náměšť) A16.592. "Sei quartetti fugati . . ." *Copyist* local? *Watermark* 3 crescents, decreasing size / A(?)M(broken)[24] / bow with arrow through it (broken)[57]
Literature	Barrett-Ayres/HAYDN p. 132 Brown/CHAMBER pp. 224, 235, 237-39, 242, 245-46, 250 Brown/QUARTETS pp. 315-18 Kirkendale/FUGE p. 123

IV: F1, B♭4, E♭1, C1, G1 and D2   2 VIOLINS, VIOLA AND BASS

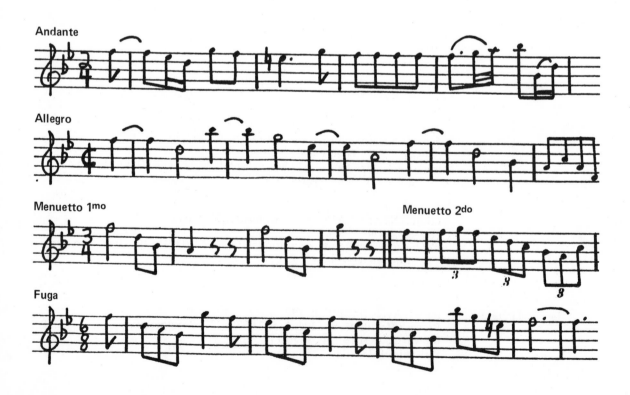

Allegro con Franchezza

Andante larghetto

Menuetto 1mo: Allegro **Menuetto 2do: Listesso tempo**

Fuga

Allegro

Menuetto 1mo: Allegro **Menuetto 2do: Allegro**

Andante

Fuga

Copies   **A-Wn** (Kaisersammlung) S.m.12163-12168. "Quartetto . . ."
Copyist   N. H., dated 1788
Watermark   Man figure, right leg forward, holding torch (?) in right hand
       (broken)[116] [double chain lines]

   A-Wn (Dr. Collins of St. Pölten) S.m.21998-21999, 22714-22715
       (only D2, E♭1, F1, and G1). "Quartetto . . . [23. Apr. 1786]"
Copyist   Viennese
Watermark   3 crescents, decreasing size[30], REAL[18] below / GFA[22]

Literature   Brown/CHAMBER   pp. 224, 235, 245-46, 248-49, 252-54, 256
   Brown/QUARTETS   p. 317
   Kirkendale/FUGE   pp. 116, 122, 142, 151, 165, 171

IV/*Q*: D1   2 VIOLINS, VIOLA AND BASS

Copy   **CS-Pnm** (Horšovský Týn) XLIX.C.505 (title page lost, only bass part extant)
Copyist   Viennese No. 4
Watermark   Eagle with heart inside and crown on top (broken)[109] /
       I HELLER (?)

Literature   Brown/CHAMBER   p. 227

IV/*S*: C1   2 VIOLINS, VIOLA AND BASS

Copy	**A-M** IV/1798 (title page lost)
Conflicting Attribution	Ignace Pleyel. See Benton/PLEYEL B. 319
Correct Author	Ignace Pleyel
Literature	Brown/CHAMBER p. 226
Remarks	The only evidence for the authorship of Ordonez is the card catalog of **A-M**. Stylistic observation does not corroborate this citation.

IV/*S*: C2   2 VIOLINS, VIOLA AND BASS

Copy	**A-M** IV/1798 (title page lost)
Literature	Brown/CHAMBER p. 226
Remarks	The only evidence for the authorship of Ordonez is the card catalog of **A-M**. Stylistic observation does not corroborate this citation.

IV/S: D1   2 VIOLINS, VIOLA AND BASS

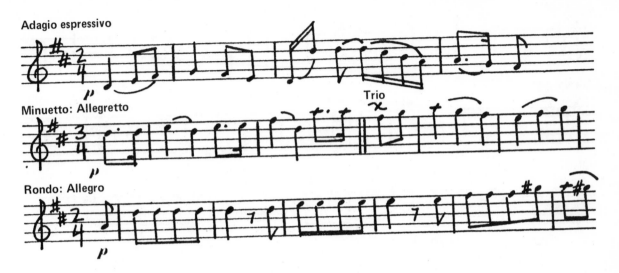

Copy	**A-M** IV/1798 (title page lost)
Conflicting Attribution	Ignace Pleyel. See Benton/PLEYEL B.324
Correct Author	Ignace Pleyel
Literature	Brown/CHAMBER p. 226
Remarks	The only evidence for the authorship of Ordonez is the card catalog of **A-M**. Stylistic observation does not corroborate this citation.

IV/S: F1   2 VIOLINS, VIOLA AND BASS

Copy	**A-M** IV/1798 (title page lost)
Conflicting Attribution	Ignace Pleyel. See Benton/PLEYEL B.321
Correct Author	Ignace Pleyel
Literature	Brown/CHAMBER p. 226
Remarks	The only evidence for the authorship of Ordonez is the card catalog of **A-M**. Stylistic observation does not corroborate this citation.

IV/S: F2   2 VIOLINS, VIOLA AND BASS

Copy	**A-M** IV/1798 (title page lost)
Literature	Brown/CHAMBER p. 226
Remarks	The only evidence for the authorship of Ordonez is the card catalog of **A-M**. Stylistic observation does not corroborate this citation.

IV/S: G1   2 VIOLINS, VIOLA AND BASS

Copy	**A-M** IV/1798 (title page lost)
Conflicting Attribution	Ignace Pleyel. See Benton/PLEYEL B.320
Correct Author	Ignace Pleyel
Literature	Brown/CHAMBER p. 226
Remarks	The only evidence for the authorship of Ordonez is the card catalog of **A-M**. Stylistic observation does not corroborate this citation.

IV/*S*: A1

Copy	**A-M** IV/1798 (title page lost)
Remarks	The only evidence for the authorship of Ordonez is the card catalog of **A-M**. Stylistic observation does not corroborate this citation. This work is not contained in the thematic index in Brown/CHAMBER.

IV/*S*: B♭1   2 VIOLINS, VIOLA AND BASS

Copy	**A-M** IV/1798 (title page lost)
Conflicting Attribution	Ignace Pleyel. See Benton/PLEYEL B.323
Correct Author	Ignace Pleyel
Literature	Brown/CHAMBER p. 226
Remarks	The only evidence for the authorship of Ordonez is the card catalog of **A-M**. Stylistic observation does not corroborate this citation.

IV/*S*: **B♭2**   2 VIOLINS, VIOLA AND BASS

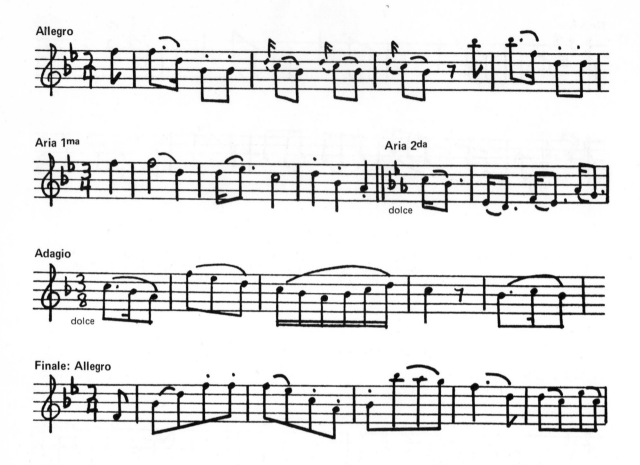

<table>
<tr><td>*Copy*</td><td>**A-Wn** S.m.12171   (title page lost)
Copyist Viennese
Watermark Eagle, I HELLER (?)</td></tr>
<tr><td>*Conflicting Attributions*</td><td>Joseph Haydn.   See Hob. III: B6 and Fuchs/HAYDN, p. 66, no. 12
Johann Vanhal.   See prints of his Op. 4/3 by Hummel (without minuet) and
        Op. 24/2 by Le Menu</td></tr>
<tr><td>*Correct Author*</td><td>Johann Vanhal</td></tr>
<tr><td>*Literature*</td><td>Brown/CHAMBER p. 224
Landon/DOUBTFUL p. 219
Landon/PROBLEMS   p. 36
Larsen/DHK   p. 126 (IX: B5)</td></tr>
</table>

IV/*S*: **B**♭**3**   2 VIOLINS, VIOLA AND BASS

Moderato

Allegretto

Copy	**A-M** IV/1798 (title page lost)
Literature	Brown/CHAMBER p. 226
Remarks	The only evidence for the authorship of Ordonez is the card catalog of **A-M**. Stylistic observation does not corroborate this citation.

Group V
STRING TRIOS

V: C1   2 VIOLINS AND BASS

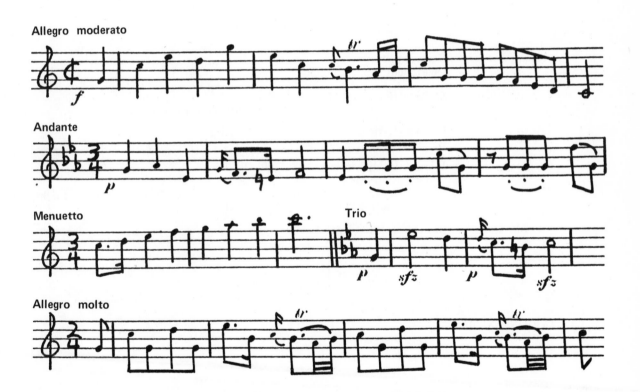

Allegro moderato

Andante

Menuetto   Trio

Allegro molto

Catalog Entry	Ringmacher 1773, p. 40
Copy	**I-Gi (l)** (Assereto?) M.4.28.23/25. "VI Sonate . . ."
	Copyists Group B
	Watermark 3 crescents, decreasing size (?) / anchor, W[31] below
Literature	Brown/ CHAMBER pp. 229, 249, 252-53, 258

V: C2 2 VIOLINS AND BASS

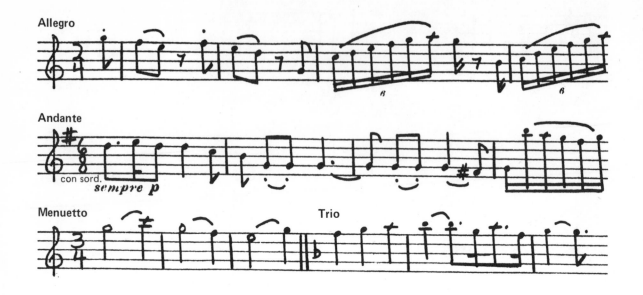

<table>
<tr><td>*Catalog Entries*</td><td>Kačina p. 46
Quartbuch I, p. 12, no. 30</td></tr>
<tr><td>*Copies*</td><td>**CS-Pnm** (Horšovský Týn) XLII.F.334. "VI Divertimenti . . ."
Watermark 3 crescents / baldachin[35] with AO (or OA?)[32] below (broken)

CS-Pnm (Kačina) XLI.C.37. "Divertimento . . ."
Watermark 3 crescents, decreasing size (?), A[17] below / AS (MS?-broken)

D-brd-B (Georg Kinsky) 16365/10. "5 Trio . . ."
Copyist German?
Watermark Coat of arms (broken-with eagle?)[108], CAMM[22] below and to right /
    G[26] with PAPPIER[22] below and to left</td></tr>
<tr><td>*Literature*</td><td>Brown/CHAMBER pp. 227-28</td></tr>
</table>

V: C3 2 VIOLINS AND BASS

Presto

Catalog Entry	Quartbuch I, p. 12, no. 29
Copy	**B-Bc** (Wagener) 14.237. "VI Sonate . . ."
	Copyists Group B
	Watermark 3 crescents, decreasing size / ornament with crown on top and W[25] inside (broken)
Literature	Brown/CHAMBER p. 229

V: **D1** 2 VIOLINS AND BASS

Allegro

Andante piu Adagio

Menuet

Catalog Entry	Quartbuch I, p. 18, no. 44
Copy	**CS-Pnm** (Horšovský Týn) XLII.F.334. "VI Divertimenti . . ."
	Watermark 3 crescents / baldachin[35] with AO (or OA?)[32] below (broken)
Literature	Brown/CHAMBER p. 227

V: D2   2 VIOLINS AND BASS

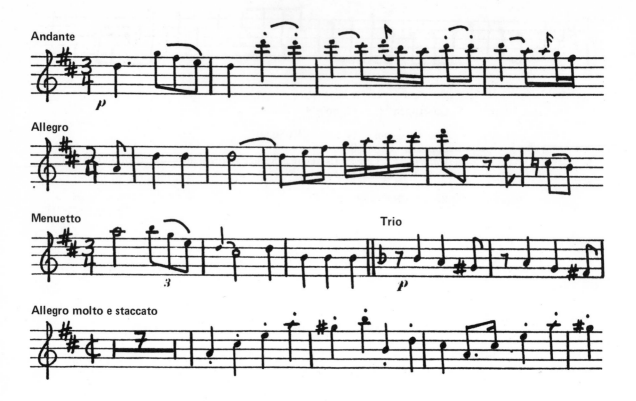

Catalog Entries	Quartbuch I, p. 18, no. 43
	Ringmacher 1773, p. 40
Copy	**I-Gi (l)** (Assereto?) M.4.28.23/25. "VI Sonate . . ."
	Copyists Group B
	Watermark 3 crescents, decreasing size (?) / anchor, W[31] below
Literature	Brown/CHAMBER pp. 229, 242-43, 258

V: D3   2 VIOLINS AND BASS

Finale: Allegro

Catalog Entry	Quartbuch I, p. 18, no. 45
Copies	**B-Bc** (Wagener) 14.237. "VI Sonate . . ."
	Copyists Group B
	Watermark 3 crescents, decreasing size / ornament with crown on top and W[25] inside (broken)
	D-brd-B (Georg Kinsky) 16365/10. "5 Trio . . ."
	Copyist German?
	Watermark Coat of arms (broken-with eagle?)[108], CAMM[22] below and to right / G[26] with PAPPIER[22] below and to left
Literature	Brown/CHAMBER pp. 228-29

V: E♭1   2 VIOLINS AND BASS

Catalog Entries	Kačina p. 46
	Quartbuch I, p. 25, no. 77
Copies	**CS-Pnm** (Horšovský Týn) XLII.F.334. "VI Divertimenti . . ."
	Watermark 3 crescents / baldachin[35] with AO (or OA?)[32] below (broken)
	CS-Pnm (Kačina) XLI.C.38. "Divertimento . . ."
	Watermark 3 crescents, decreasing size (?), A[17] below / AS (MS?-broken)
Literature	Brown/CHAMBER p. 227

V: E♭2   2 VIOLINS AND BASS

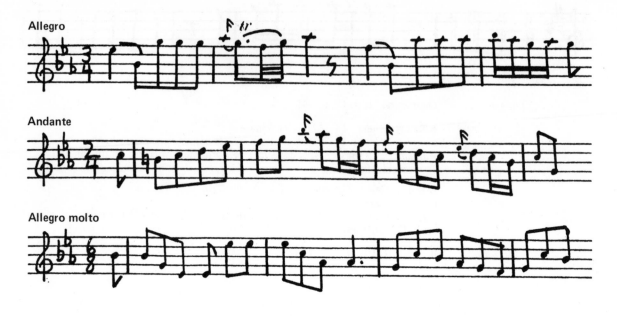

Catalog Entries	Melk V, no. 100
	Quartbuch I, p. 25, no. 76
Copies	**A-M** V/100. "Trio . . ."
	Copyist Viennese
	Watermark Baldachin[47] with GF[37] below / ornament with 3 six-pointed stars inside and crescent on top[182]
	B-Bc (Wagener) 14.237. "VI Sonate . . ."
	Copyists Group B
	Watermark 3 crescents, decreasing size / ornament with crown on top and W[25] inside (broken)
Literature	Brown/CHAMBER pp. 224-25, 229

V: E♭3   2 VIOLINS AND BASS

Tempo di Menuetto

Copy	**I-Gi (l)** (Assereto?) M.4.28.23/25. "VI Sonate . . ."
	Copyists Group B
	Watermark 3 crescents, decreasing size (?) / anchor, W^{31} below
Literature	Brown/CHAMBER pp. 229, 249

V: F1 2 VIOLINS AND BASS

Andante

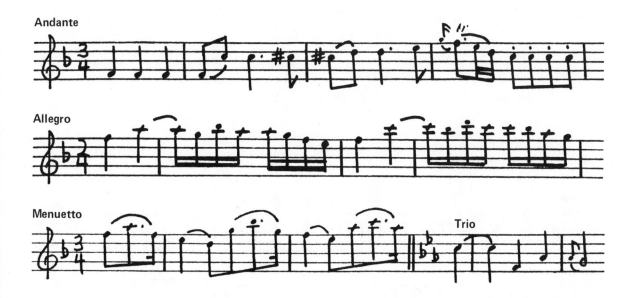

Allegro

Menuetto   **Trio**

Catalog Entry	Quartbuch I, p. 28, no. 31
Copies	**B-Bc** (Wagener) 14.237. "VI Sonate . . ."
	Copyists Group B
	Watermark 3 crescents, decreasing size / ornament with crown on top and W^{25} inside (broken)
	D-brd-B (Georg Kinsky) 16365/10. "5 Trio . . ."
	Copyist German?
	Watermark Coat of arms (broken-with eagle?)[108], $CAMM^{22}$ below and to right / G^{26} with $PAPPIER^{22}$ below and to left
Literature	Brown/CHAMBER pp. 228-29, 242-43

V: **F2**   2 VIOLINS AND BASS

| *Catalog Entries* | Quartbuch I, p. 28, no. 33 |
| | Ringmacher 1773, p. 39 |

Copies   **CS-Pnm** (Horšovský Týn) XLII.F.334. "VI Divertimenti . . ."
Watermark 3 crescents / baldachin[35] with AO (or OA?)[32] below (broken)

H-KE (Festetics) KO/56. "Divertimento . . ."
Copyist Viennese
Watermark 3 crescents, decreasing size[41], REAL (?-broken)[22] below / baldachin
(?-broken)[29], AS[33] below

Literature   Brown/CHAMBER   pp. 227-28, 232

V: **F3**   2 VIOLINS AND BASS

Copy   **A-Gi (l)** (Assereto?) M.4.28.23/25. "VI Sonate . . ."
Copyists Group B
Watermark 3 crescents, decreasing size (?) / anchor, W[31] below

Literature   Brown/CHAMBER   pp. 229, 243, 246

V: F4   2 VIOLINS AND BASS

Copy   **A-M** V/99. "Divertimento . . ."
            Copyist Viennese
            Watermark Baldachin[47] with GF[37] below / ornament with 3 six-pointed
            stars inside and crescent on top[182]

Literature   Brown/CHAMBER pp. 225, 248-49, 254-55

V: G1   2 VIOLINS AND BASS

Catalog Entry   Ringmacher 1773, p. 40

Copy   **I-Gi(l)** (Assereto?) M.4.28.23/25. "VI Sonate . . ."
            Copyists Group B
            Watermark 3 crescents, decreasing size (?) / anchor, W[31] below

Literature   Brown/CHAMBER pp. 229, 250

V: G2   2 VIOLINS AND BASS

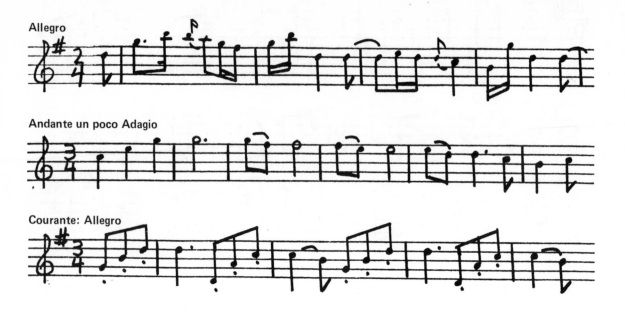

Allegro

Andante un poco Adagio

Courante: Allegro

Catalog Entry	Quartbuch I, p. 33, no. 51
Copies	**B-Bc** (Wagener) 14.237. "VI Sonate . . ." *Copyists* Group B *Watermark* 3 crescents, decreasing size / ornament with crown on top and W[25] inside (broken)
	D-brd-B (Georg Kinsky) 16365/10. "5 Trio . . ." *Copyist* German? *Watermark* Coat of arms (broken-with eagle?)[108] , CAMM[22] below and to right / G[26] with **PAPPIER**[22] below and to left
Literature	Brown/CHAMBER pp. 228-29

V: A1   2 VIOLINS AND BASS

Allegro moderato

Adagio

Menuetto: Lento

Copy **A-M** V/98. "Divertimento . . ."
Copyist Viennese
Watermark Baldachin[47] with GF[37] below / ornament with 3 six-pointed stars
   inside and crescent on top[182]

Literature Brown/CHAMBER pp. 225, 258

V: A2 2 VIOLINS AND BASS

Allegro moderato

Andantino

Allegro moderato

Catalog Entry Ringmacher 1773, p. 39

Copies **A-Wn** S.m. 12638. "Sixime Entretien . . ."
Copyist Viennese
Watermarks 3 crescents, decreasing size, REAL (?) / primitive flower with $\frac{CS}{C}$
   below; 3 crescents / A (or AS?); 3 crescents, REAL / AS

I-Gi(l) (Assereto?) M.4.28.23/25. "VI Sonate . . ."
Copyists Group B
Watermark 3 crescents, decreasing size (?) / anchor, W[31] below

Literature Brown/CHAMBER p. 229

V: A3   2 VIOLINS AND BASS

Catalog Entry	Quartbuch I, p. 4, no. 39
Copy	**B-Bc** (Wagener) 14.237. "VI Sonate . . ."
	Copyists Group B
	Watermark 3 crescents, decreasing size / ornament with crown on top and W^{25} inside (broken)
Literature	Brown/CHAMBER p. 229

V: A4   2 VIOLINS AND BASS

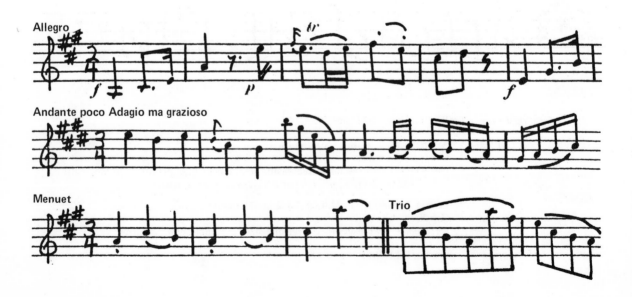

Catalog Entry	Quartbuch I, p. 3, no. 38
Copy	**CS-Pnm** (Horšovský Tín) XLII.F.334. "VI Divertimenti ..." *Watermark* 3 crescents / baldachin[35] with AO (or OA?)[32] below (broken)
Literature	Brown/CHAMBER p. 227

V: B♭1 2 VIOLINS AND BASS

Copy	**D-ddr-Dlb** (Braunschweig-Oels) Mus.3315-Q-1. "Divertimento ..." *Copyist* Viennese No. 6
Literature	Brown/CHAMBER p. 228

V: B♭2 2 VIOLINS AND BASS

Catalog Entries	Kačina p. 46
	Quartbuch I, p. 9, no. 48

Copies	**CS-Pnm** (Horšovský Týn) XLII.F.334. "VI Divertimenti . . ."
	Watermark 3 crescents / baldachin[35] with AO (or OA?)[32] below (broken)
	CS-Pnm (Kačina) XLI.C.39. "Divertimento . . ."
	Watermark 3 crescents, decreasing size (?), A[17] below / AS (MS?-broken)
	D-brd-B (Georg Kinsky) 16365/10. "5 Trio . . ."
	Copyist German?
	Watermark Coat of arms (broken-with eagle?)[108], CAMM[22] below and to right / G[26] with PAPPIER[22] below and to left

Literature	Brown/CHAMBER pp. 227-28

V/*Q*: G1   VIOLIN, VIOLA AND BASS

Copy	**A-Wgm** (Leopold Sonnleithner) IX/23420. "Divertimento . . ." ("Ordonez" added in pencil.)
	Copyist Viennese No. 6
	Watermark Coat of arms with crown on top, anchor (?) in left half[91] / ЅB[29]

Literature	Brown/CHAMBER p. 225

V/Q: A♭1   SOLO VIOLA, VIOLIN AND CELLO

Copy	**A-Wgm** (Leopold Sonnleithner) IX/23420. "Divertimento . . ." ("Ordonez" added in pencil.)
	Copyist Viennese No. 6
	Watermark Crown with cross above[97], WALDS[20] ZEL[20] below FCS[24]

Literature	Brown/CHAMBER pp. 225, 239

V/S: E♭1   VIOLIN, VIOLA AND BASS

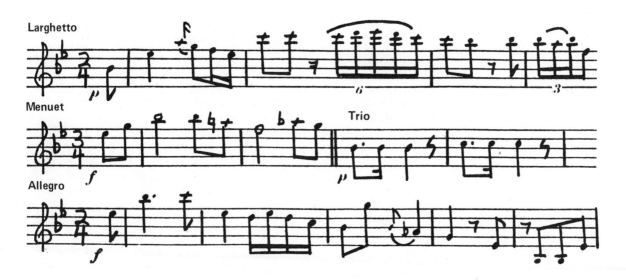

Copy	**A-Wgm** (Leopold Sonnleithner) IX/23419. "Divertimento Notturno . . ." ("Ordonez" in pencil on cover, "Amandus Ivanschutz" inscribed by copyist on underfold of cover.)
	Copyist Viennese No. 6
	Watermark Papageno-like man figure, right leg forward (broken)[99] / ERW (FRW?)
Correct Author	Amandus Ivanschutz. See Breitkopf catalog for 1767, col. 279
Literature	Brown/CHAMBER p. 225

V/S: G1 2 VIOLINS AND BASS

Adagio

Un poco Presto

Tempo di Menuet

Copy	**A-Wgm** (Leopold Sonnleithner) IX/23420. "Divertimento . . ." ("Ordonez" in pencil on cover, "Haydn" inscribed by copyist on underfold of cover.)
	Copyist Viennese
	Watermarks Coat of arms (broken)[102] / IGF (?); Crown with cross above[97], WALDS[20]
	    ZEL[20] below
	    FCS[24]

Correct Author	Joseph Haydn. See Hob. V: G4; Quartbuch, I, p. 31, no. 26; **CS-Pnm**-Pachta XXII-D-26. "Divertimento . . ." *Copyist* Viennese
Literature	Brown/CHAMBER p. 225 Brown/ INTRODUCTION Landon/ PROBLEMS p. 36 Larsen/DHK p. 125 (V: G5) Unverricht/TRIOS p. 71

Group VI
DUOS

VI: D1   VIOLIN AND BASS

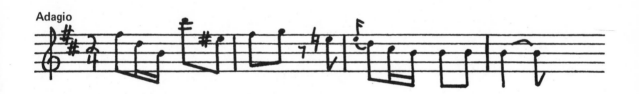

Copy	**A-Wgm** Q16719 (old IX/1018). "Sonata . . ."
	Copyist Viennese No. 1
	Watermark 3 crescents / thin (?) ornament[101] on chain line with F (?) on
	lower left, C (?)[39] on lower right (broken)

| *Literature* | Brown/CHAMBER   pp. 225, 251-52 |

VI: E♭1   VIOLIN AND BASS

Copy	**A-Wgm** Q16720 (old IX/1018). "Sonata . . ."
	Copyist Viennese No. 1
	Watermark 3 crescents / thin (?) ornament[101] on chain line with F (?) on lower left, C (?)[39] on lower right (broken)
Literature	Brown/CHAMBER pp. 225, 236, 243

VI: U1-3   2 VIOLINS

Catalog Entry	Traeg 1799, p. 87, no. 39 ("3 Duetti . . .")

Group VII
VOCAL WORKS

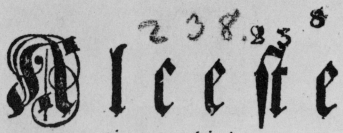

Alceste

ein parodirt=
Gesungenes Trauerspiel
in drey Aufzügen.
Bey Gelegenheit
Der höchst=erfreulichen Gegenwart
Ihrer königlichen Hoheiten
des
Durchlauchtigsten Erzherzogs
Ferdinand,
und Allerhöchst=Dero
Durchlauchtigsten Gemahlinn
Beatrice, von Este,
in einer
Marionetten Operette zum erstenmale
zu Esterház
Auf der fürstlichen Marionetten Bühne
im Jahre 1775. aufgeführet.

Oedenburg, gedruckt bey Johann Joseph Sieß.

Title page of
libretto for
1775 Esterháza
performance
of *Alceste*

VIIa: 1 MARIONETTE OPERA. MUSICA DELLA PARODIA d'ALCESTE.   Libretto by Karl von Pauersbach

SINFONIA

ACT I

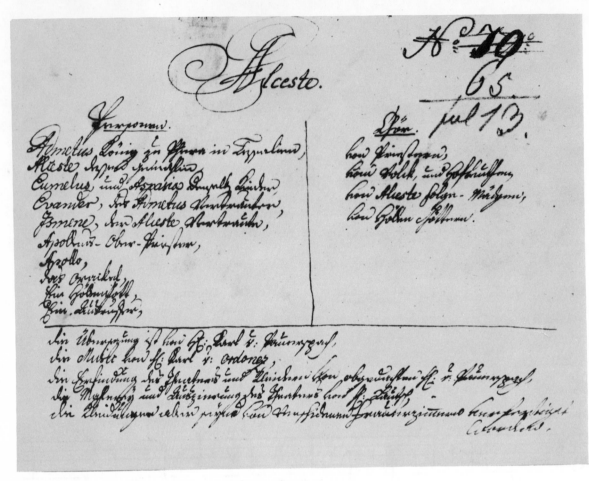

Title page of *Alceste* from the copy owned by Joseph Haydn

Adagio un poco Andante

Ich for — dere nicht ihr e — wi — ge Göt — ter

Menuetto in Tempo Comodo e piano

Moderato

Wir bit — ten dich de — mu — thig — lich.

Andante

Der Kö — nig stirbt ge — wiss

Allegro

Ganz g'hor — sam — er Die — ner

Adagio

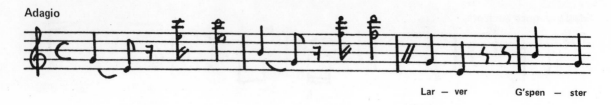

Lar — ver G'spen — ster

[Allegro]

Nicht al — les,

was glän — zet ist Sil — ber und Gold.

ACT II

Andante

Ich geh'

Andante

doch doch

Adagio

O Hien — zinn dum — mer

Hau — ben — stock

Adagio

In — gre — de — re! du zrupf — te Waar! Kom!

Andante

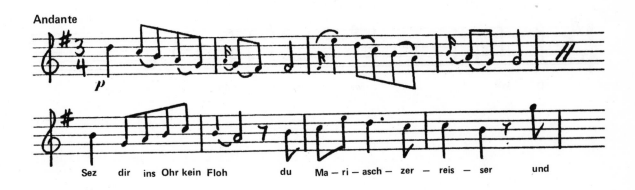

Sez dir ins Ohr kein Floh du Ma — ri — asch — zer — reis — ser und

Allegro

Flieht fin — ste — re Sor — gen

Andante

Nein du Höp — pinn ich kann nicht lie — ben.

Tempo di Menuetto ma Andante

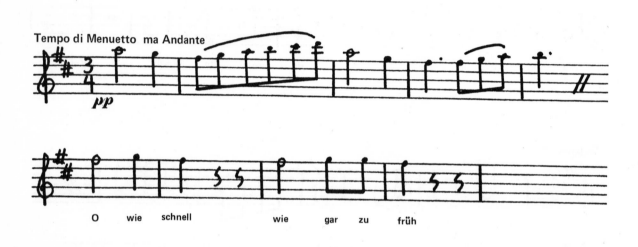

pp

O wie schnell wie gar zu früh

Andante

f   *p*   Ge — lieb — te

Kin — der   eu — er Schmerz

ACT III

[SINFONIA]

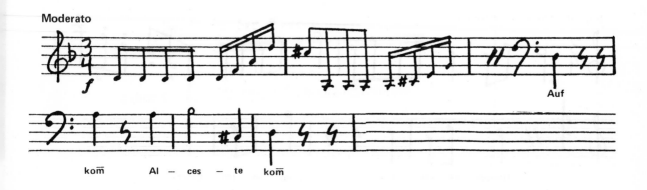

Catalog Entries	HBV No. 215
	HNV No. 557

Copy   **H-Bn** OE 65 (old Ms. Mus. IV.497). "Alceste . . ."
Copyists Viennese and Ordonez (?)
Watermarks 3 crescents, decreasing size[34], M[18] below / AS[26]; Ornament with crescent on top, 3 six-pointed stars inside[180] / ornament with crescent on top, AF inside[180]; Baldachin with crescent on top (broken)[90]

Librettos   Alceste / ein parodirt= / Gesungenes Trauerspiel / in drey Aufzügen. / Bey Gelegenheit / Der höchst=erfreulichen Gegenwart / Ihrer königlichen Hoheiten / des / Durchlauchtigsten Erzherzogs / Ferdinand, / und Allerhöchst= Dero / Durchlauchtigsten Gemahlinn / Beatrice, von Este, / in einer / Marionetten Operette zum erstenmale / zu Esterház / Auf der fürstlichen Marionetten Bühne / im Jahre 1775. aufgeführet. / / Oedenburg, gedruckt bey Johann Joseph Siess.
Location **A-Wst**

Gesänge / zur / Alceste. / Einer lustigen Opera Seria / in drey Aufzügen / nach dem Italienischen des Hrn. Calsabigi. / Aufgeführt in dem k. k. privil. Schauspiel= / hause in der Leopoldstadt. / / Wien, / gedruckt bey Mathias Andreas Schmidt.
Location **A-Wn**

Modern Edition   Tina L. Bankston. "A Transcription and Translation of 'Musica Della Parodia d'Alceste,' by Carlos d'Ordonez." Master's thesis, North Texas State University (Denton), 1972.

Literature   Bartha/ BRIEFE p. 12
Bartha-Somfai/HAYDN p. 391
BESCHREIBUNG pp. 38-40
Brown/CHAMBER p. 229
Brown/INTRODUCTION
Geiringer/HAYDN p. 295
Hadamowsky/LEOPOLDSTADT
Landon/CCLN p. vii
Landon/MARIONETTE pp. 189-90
Pohl/HAYDN II, p. 93
Sonnleithner/MATERIALIEN
WD 1775, no. 74; 1777, nos. 56-57

VIIa: 2 SINGSPIEL. DIESMAL HAT DER MANN DEN WILLEN! Libretto by J. F. Schmidt

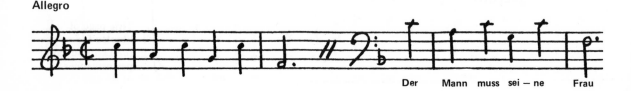

Diesmal hat der Mann den Willen!

Ein Originalsingspiel

in

einem Aufzuge.

Aufgeführt auf der k. k. Nationalschaubühne.

Die Musik ist vom Herrn Ordonez.

WIEN,

zu finden bey dem Logenmeister.

1778.

Title page of libretto for *Diesmal hat der Mann den Willen!*

Andantino

Siehst du die Täub — chen spie — len, so glau — be nur, sie füh — len

Allegretto un poco Andante

Al — les fes — selt Al — les fes — selt Al — les fes — selt

Moderato

Kutsch und Pfer — de Kutsch und Pfer — de

Allegro

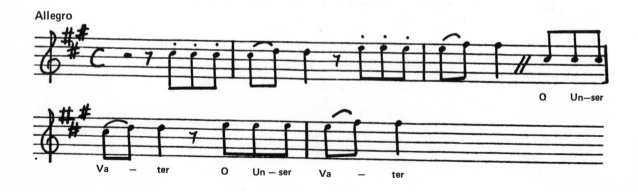

O Un—ser Va — ter O Un—ser Va — ter

Copies	**A-Wn** 16148 (score). "Diesmal hat der Mann Willen . . ."

Copyist Viennese
Watermarks 3 crescents, decreasing size / ornament (broken) with W inside
and crown on top; 3 crescents, decreasing size, REAL (?-broken) below
and off-center to left / ornament with W inside and crown on top (broken)

A-Wn 15632 (string parts only)
Copyist Viennese

Libretto Diesmal hat der Mann / den Willen! / Ein Originalsingspiel / in / einem Aufzuge. /
Aufgeführt auf der k. k. Nationalschaubühne. / Die Musik ist vom Herrn Ordonez. / /
WIEN, / zu finden bey dem Logenmeister. / 1778.
Locations **A-Wn, US-NYp, US-Wc**

Literature ATA
Brown / INTRODUCTION
Gerber / 1792 p. 46
Michtner / BURGTHEATER pp. 42-43, 360-61
Pollheimer / PAUERSBACH
WD 1778, no. 33

Remarks Music survives for only five of the twenty numbers indicated in the libretto,
as shown below (with asterisks):

Scene 1
*Duet - Rebhun, Anne and Chorus. "Der Mann muss seine Frau regieren"
Aria - Anne. "Ich will dich führen!"
Aria - Rebhun. "Wie sie kocht! wie sie schwillt!"
Duet - Rebhun, Anne and Chorus. "Der Mann muss seine Frau regieren"

Scene 2
Aria - Rose. "Lebe wohl du kleiner Wald"

Scene 3
*Duet - Rose and Blumbeck. "Siehst du die Täubchen spielen"
Aria - Blumbeck. "O was bin ich"
Aria - Rose. "Süsslokend tönt der Zitterklang"

Scene 4
Aria - Anne. "O hättest du geseh'n"

Scene 5
Aria - Flink. "Der Schnee, die Lilie zarter Wangen"
Aria - Rose. "Wir sehn den schlanken Rosmarin"
*Duet - Rose and Flink. "Alles sesselt hier das Herz!"
Ariette - Flink. "Mit diesem Thurme krönen"
*Aria - Flink. "Kutsch und Pferde — höre wohl!"
Aria - Rose. "Einem Mädchen zu Gefallen"

Scene 6
Aria - Blumbeck. "Es pocht in mir das junge Herz"

Scene 7
Aria - Graf. "Den Reiz der Liebe zu empfinden"

Scene 8
*Trio - Rose, Blumbeck and Graf. "O Unser Vater! Unser Freund!"

Scene 9
Vaudeville Chorus - "Ihr ländlichen Mädchen"

Der alte wienerische Tandelmarkt.

Mit vier Stimmen.

In Musique gesetzt

von

Karl von Ordonez.

Im Jahr 1779.

Title page of libretto for *Der alte wienerische Tandelmarkt*

VIIb: 1   CANTATA. DER ALTE WIENERISCHE TANDELMARKT

Libretto	Der alte wienerische / Tandelmarkt. / Mit vier Stimmen. / In Musique gesetzt / von / Karl von Ordonez. / Im Jahr 1779.

Location **A-Wst**

Literature	Brown/ INTRODUCTION
Remarks	A list of the musical numbers follows:

Chorus - Sagfailer. "Sagfailen, Messer schleifen"
          Hollohipen Kramer. "Herben, herben"
          Savoiard. "Schöne Raritaet"
          Arzt. "Pillen! goldene Pillen"

Aria - Sagfailer. "Sagfalla diese schöne Kunst"

Aria - Savoiard. "Schöne Raritaet / Citto guck guck"

Aria - Savoiard. "O bella Margarita!"

Aria - Hollohipen Kramer. "Allo frisch auf, gewürfelt drauf"

Aria - Arzt. "Hier hab ich eine Pille"

Aria - Savoiard. "O che bella tortorella!"

Aria - Arzt. "Ist etwa ein betagte Frau"

Aria - Hollohipen Kramer. "Aens bit i mir dö aus"

Chorus (*da Capo*)

REFERENCES TO WORKS
WHICH
CANNOT BE IDENTIFIED

GROUP I / SYMPHONIES

Copies Auction list for December 1762 [February 1763]. **S-Sk**, OKAT Bokaukt.
See Walin/SINFONIK, p. 202
   "2 Simphonier af Ordonez"

Eight symphonies in collection of Maximilian Hamilton. *See* Sehnal/
HAMILTON, p. 413

Wienerisches Diarium, (1771), Nro. 22
   "Bey Simon Haschke . . . zu haben: Eine Quantität Sinfonien, als von
   Hern. Ordenitz. . ."

Traeg catalog for 1799, p. 18
   "Ordonez (Carl.) a 2v. 2ob. 2cor. viola e B. 1 in B, 2 in Es, 3 in F,
   4 in A, 6 in D"
   [*Note:* "5 in cm" has been identified as **I: C14**]

One symphony at Spišská Kapitula for strings a 3, 2 oboes, 2 clarini and
timpani. *See* Múdra/SPIŠSKÁ KAPITULA, p. 140

Prints Venier catalog for 1765. *See* Johansson/FRENCH, facs. 120
   "Sinfonie Periodique No. 26"
   [*Note:* Boyer republished the Venier series in 1788. *See* Johansson/
   FRENCH, facs. 101]

L'Avantcoureur (Paris), (1769), Nro. 32
   "Dune & Ordonne, Trois Symphonies à deux Violons, alto & Basse, &
   deux Cors ad libitum, mis au jour & gravées par Mlle Vendôme & le
   Sr Moria, rue des Fossés M. le Prince vis-à-vis le Riche Laboureur. 61.
   Paris, aux adr. ord. de Mus. Lyon, chez Castaud place de la Comédie,
   & à Rouen chez Magoy, rue des Carmes"

Performance Advertisement for Tonkünstler Societät concert, 17 März 1777. *See also*
Pohl/DENKSCHRIFT, p. 58
   "Eine neue, grosse Sinfonie von der Erfindung des Herrn von Ordonez"

GROUP III / DIVERTIMENTI, ETC., FOR 8 TO 5 PARTS

Prints   Bureau d'abonnement Musical catalog for 1769. *See* Johansson/FRENCH, facs. 17
"Ordonez   Gasse 3"
[*Note:* The other two works in the series are by Dittersdorf (Krebs Nos. 132 and 134). The Ordonez print was at one time a part of the collection of **D-ddr-B** (mus.17613) but is no longer extant]

Westphal catalog for 1782, p. 20
"Ordonez . . . Op.3 a5 p. Violino, Alto, 2 Corni et Basso . . ."

GROUP IV / QUARTETS

Copies   Traeg catalog for 1799, p. 66
"6 Quartetti, 6 Quartetti"

Print   Westphal catalog for 1782, p. 27
"Differens Auteurs, 6 Quat. No.1 a6. 2 Viol. Alt e Bass, davon 2 von Godécharle, 2 von d'Ordonez & 2 von J. Schmitt . . . Brüssel"

GROUP V / TRIOS

Copy   Morales/COBBETT'S
". . . six trios for 2 violins and bass (Strahe Library, Giessen) . . ."

TRACINGS OF
DATABLE WATERMARKS

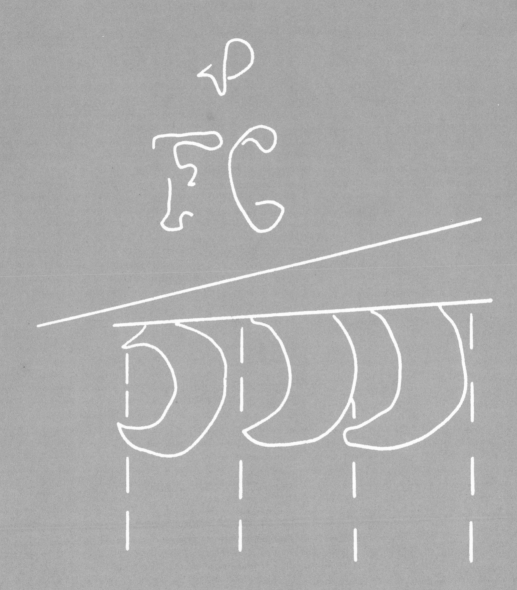

Date: 1758.   A-GÖ (IIc: 2)

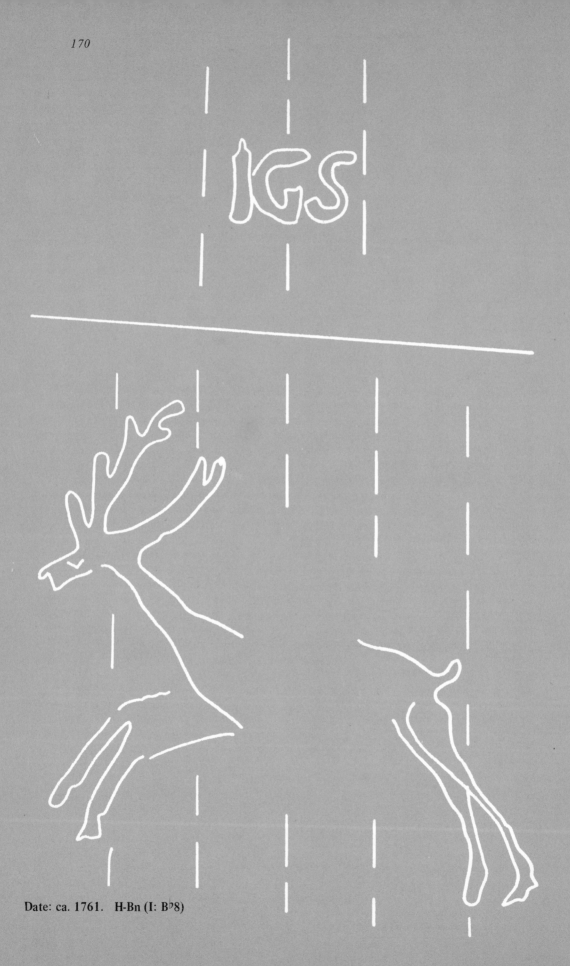

Date: ca. 1761.   H-Bn (I: B♭8)

Date: 1763. A-GÖ (IIIc: F2)

172

Date: 1764.   A-GÖ (I: A6, I: B♭1)

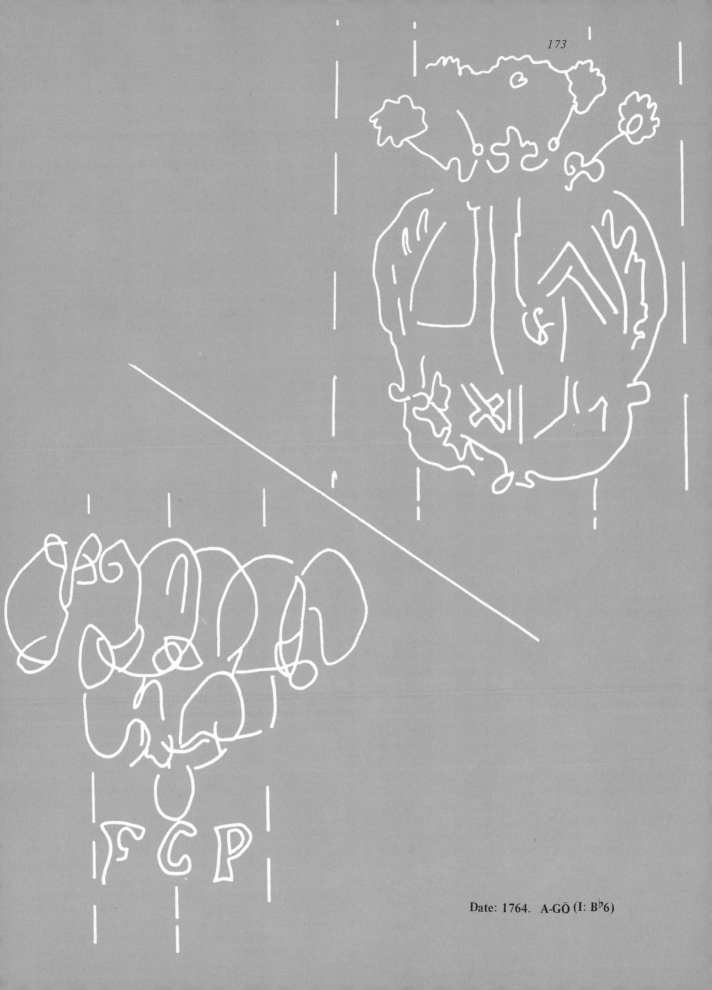

Date: 1764. A-GÖ (I: B♭6)

Date: before 1768.   A-LA (I: D2)

Date: before 1768.   A-LA (I: D8, I: F11, I: B♭8)

Date: ca. 1769?
D-ddr-Bds-Königliche Hausbibliothek
(IV: F4 and B♭3, Opus 2)

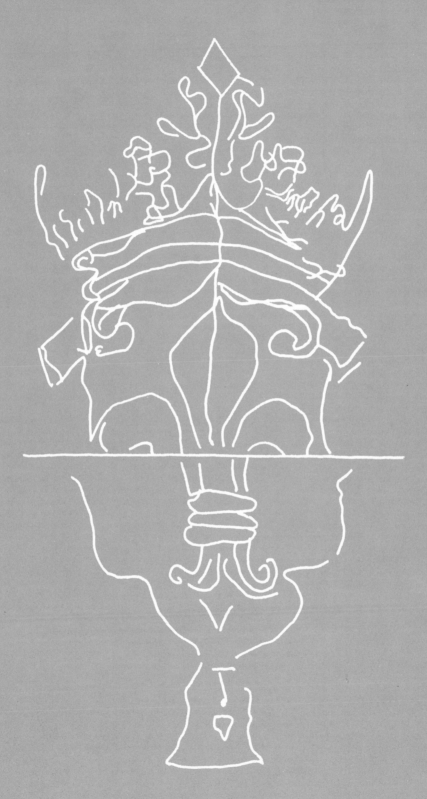

Date: 1772. D-brd-DO (I: A8)
[schematic representation only]

Date: 1775.   H-Bn (VIIa: 1)

Date: 1775.   H-Bn (VIIa: 1)

Date: 1775.   H-Bn (VIIa: 1)

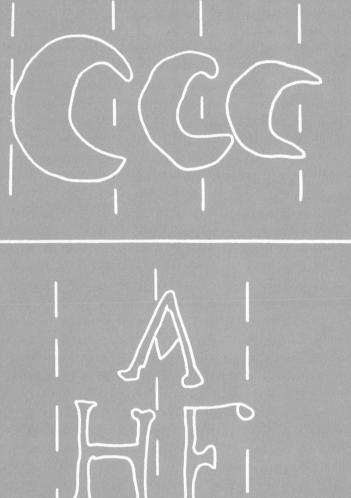

Date: 1777. A-Wpfannhauser (I: D7)

Date: 1779.   CS-Bm-Rajhrad (I: D6, I: B♭4)

Date: 1786. A-Wn-Kaisersammlung (Opus 1)

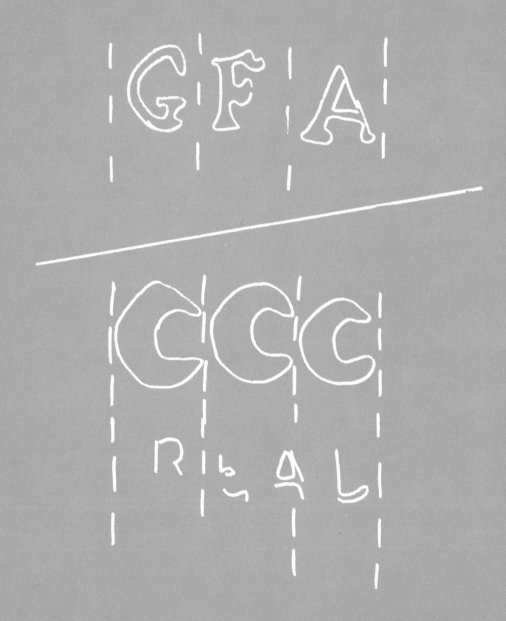

Date: 1786.   A-Wn-Kaisersammlung (Opus 1, Opus 2)

Date: 1786.   A-Wn-Kaisersammlung (Opus 2)

Date: 1788.   A-Wn-Kaisersammlung (IV: F1, B♭4, E♭1, C1, G1 and D2)

Date: 1788.   A-Wn-Kaisersammlung (IV: G3, D1, C2, A2, F2 and D3)

FACSIMILES OF
SELECTED COPYISTS

Group A, Copyist 1.   I: C5, 1st mvt, Clarino 1.   I-MOe

Group A, Copyist 1.   I: C8, 1st mvt, Bass.   I-MOe

Group A, Copyist 2 (= Viennese No. 2). I: C8, 1st mvt, Violin 1. I-MOe

194

Group A, Copyist 2 (= Viennese No. 2). I: C10, 1st mvt, Bass. I-MOe

Group A, Copyist 3.   I: C10, 1st mvt, Violin 1.   I-MOe

Group A, Copyist 3.   I: F4, 1st mvt, Bass.   I-MOe

Group A, Copyist 4.   I: B♭3, 1st mvt, Violin 1.   I-MOe

Group A, Copyist 5.   I: E♭5, Title page.   I-MOe

Group A, Copyist 5.   I: E♭5, 1st mvt, Bass.   I-MOe

Muda Prima

N.° VI

3. Sonate

A Due Violini e Basso

Del Sig: Carlo D' Ordonez

Violino Primo

Group B, Copyist 1.   V: C3, D3, E♭2, F1, G2, A3, Title page.   B-Bc

Group B, Copyist 1.   V: C3, 1st mvt, Violin 1.   B-Bc

Group B, Copyist 2.   I: F1, 1st mvt, Violin 1.   I-Gi(1)

Group B, Copyist 3.   I: C9, 3rd mvt, Violin 1.   I-Gi(1)

Sei Sonate
Per due Violini,
Viola e Violoncello
Del Signor
Carlo d'Ordonez

Violoncello

Group B, Copyist 4.   Opus 2, Title page.   I-Gi(1)

Group B, Copyist 4. IV: F4, 2nd mvt, Violin 2. I-Gi(1)

Group B, Copyist 5.   IV: C3, 2nd mvt, Violin 1.   I-Gi(1)

VI Sonate
A due Violini e Violoncello
Del Sig.
Carlo d'Ordonez

Violino Primo

Group B, Copyist 6.   V: C1, D2, E♭3, F3, G1, A2, Title page.   I-Gi(1)

15

Group B, Copyist 6.   V: D2, 1st mvt, Violin 1.   I-Gi(1)

Group B, Copyist 7.   IV: G2, 4th mvt, Violin 1.   H-Bn

No. 7

Quartetto in E moll

à
2 Violini

Viola

e Basso

Del Sigr. Carlo d'Ordonez

Andante

N. H. IV: E♭2, 1st mvt, Violin 1. A-Wn

Above and overleaf:
Johann Schmutzer. I: F3, 1st mvt, Violin 1. I-MOe

Johann Schmutzer. I: F3, continuation of 1st mvt, Violin 1. I-MOe

Q 16720

Viennese No. 1.   VI: E♭1, Title page.   A-Wgm

Viennese No. 1.   VI: E♭1, 1st mvt, Violin.   A-Wgm

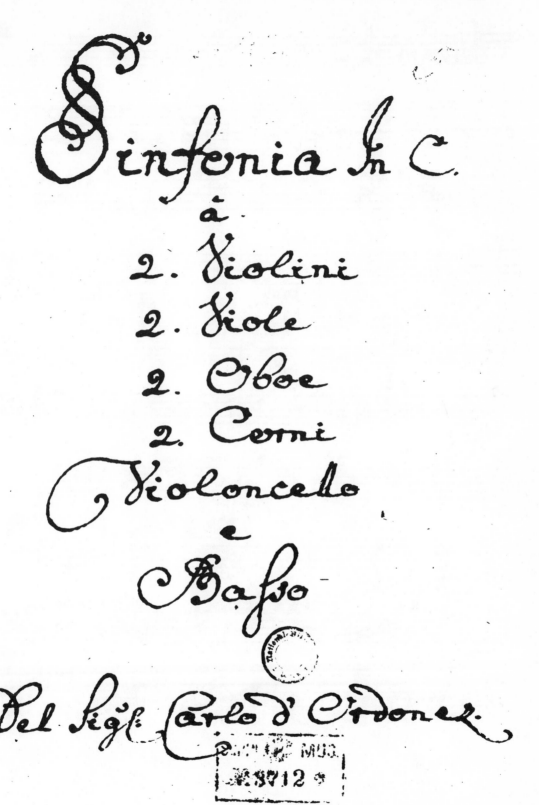

Sinfonia in C.
à
2. Violini
2. Viole
2. Oboe
2. Corni
Violoncelo
e
Basso

Del Sig.r Carlo d'Ordonez.

Viennese No. 4. I: C7, Title page. A-Wn

Viennese No. 4.   I: C7, 1st mvt, Violin 1.   A-Wn

220

Viennese No. 5.   IV: C4, 1st mvt, Violin 1.   CS-K

Viennese No. 6.   V: B♭1, 1st mvt, Violin 1.   D-ddr-Dlb

Above and overleaf:
Viennese No. 7.   I: C14, 1st mvt, Violin 1.   I-Fc

224

Viennese No. 7.   I: C14, continuation of 1st mvt, Violin 1.   I-Fc

INDEX

INDEX OF WATERMARKS

*The watermarks are indexed in their entirety under the first described element, and by each associated element; e.g., "Baldachin with GF below" is indexed in its entirety under **BALDACHIN**, and the associated element "GF" is indexed under **LETTERS**. Reference is made to the catalog number of a work which has a listed copy containing the watermark. References to a single associated element—as opposed to an entire watermark—are identified by parentheses around the catalog number. Exponents refer to the number of copies containing the watermark under the given catalog number.*

ANCHOR
   Anchor: (I: D10) (I: B♭6) (V/Q: G1?)
   Anchor, W below: I: C8 I: D4 I: D7 I: F2 I: G3 V: C1 V: D2 V: E♭3 V: F3 V: G1 V: A2

ANIMAL
   Bird: I: E♭3 I: E♭4 I: E1 I: F1 I: G5 I: A6 I: B♭5. *See also* **EAGLE**
   Horse(?): I: C9
   Lion(?) on hind legs, forelegs on oval with $_A^F{}_W$ inside: I: D8 I: F11 I: B♭8
   Stag, large, jumping: I: B♭8
   Stag, small, jumping: I: F9
   Unicorn. *See* Horse(?)

BALDACHIN
   Baldachin: (I: E♭1) (I: B♭5) Opus 1?
   Baldachin with AO(or OA?) below: V: C2 V: D1 V: E♭1 V: F2 V: A4 V: B♭2
   Baldachin (?) with AS below: V: F2
   Baldachin(?) with GB below: Opus 1
   Baldachin with GF below: I: C7 I: D6 I: D7 I: F5 I: G7 I: B♭4 I: B1 Opus 1 Opus 2 V: E♭2
      V: F4 V: A1
   Baldachin with crescent on top: I: C9² VIIa: 1
   Baldachin with crescent on top, GF below: I: C10 I: C14 I: E♭1 I: E4 Opus 1

BELL
  Bell with visible clapper: (I: A8)

LETTERS

A: I: C8 (I: E$\flat$4) (V: C2) (V: E$\flat$1) (V: B$\flat$2)

A (or AS?): V: A2

$\begin{smallmatrix}A\\HF\\REAL\end{smallmatrix}$: I: D7

AB?: Opus 1

ADLER(?), IPR(?) below, indecipherable object above: I: E$\flat$5 I: A6

AF: (VIIa: 1)

AFC: (I: E$\flat$1) (I: B$\flat$5)

AH (EISLER or HEILIG?): Opus 2

ALLEMODEPAPEIR (?): (I: C8^2) (I: D1) (I: D9) (I: E$\flat$5) (I: F12) (I: G5) (I: A1) (I: A4) (I: A6) (I: A8)

AM: IV: F4 IV: B$\flat$3 Opus 1 Opus 2 IV: C2? IV: D1? IV: D3? IV: F2? IV: G3 IV: A2

AO (or OA?): (V: C2) (V: D1) (V: E$\flat$1) (V: F2) (V: A4) (V: B$\flat$2)

AS: I: C10 I: C12 I: E1? I: F2 I: F6 I: G8 (V: F2) V: A2 VIIa: 1

AS(MS?): V: C2 V: E$\flat$1 V: B$\flat$2

ASF(?): (I: D10) (I: B$\flat$6)

AW: (I: D8) (I: F11) (I: B$\flat$8)

$\begin{smallmatrix}AZ.\\C\end{smallmatrix}$: (I: C9)

?B: (I: F8)

B_D: (I: C8)

B?UB: (I: A1)

BVBG(?): I: E$\flat$3

BVT inside rectangular frame(?): I: C1 I: F11 I: G2 I: A7 I: A10

C: (I: C9) (I: B$\flat$5) (Opus 1^2)

CAMM: (V: C2) (V: D3) (V: F1) (V: G2) (V: B$\flat$2)

CF: I: C9?^{2} I: F12

$\begin{smallmatrix}CG\\C\end{smallmatrix}$(?): (I:C10) (I: F4)

$\begin{smallmatrix}CS.\\C\end{smallmatrix}$: (I: C2) (I: E$\flat$1?) (I: F4?) (I: B$\flat$2?) (I/*S*: C2) (V: A2)

ERW (FRW?): V/*S*: E$\flat$1

$\begin{smallmatrix}F\\A\,W\end{smallmatrix}$: (I: D8) (I: F11) (I: B$\flat$8)

$\begin{smallmatrix}F\,A.\\G\end{smallmatrix}$: (I: C10)

FC (?): (I: B$\flat$5) (IV: A4) (VI: D1) (VI: E$\flat$1)

F (?)CP: (I: A6) (I: B$\flat$3) (I: B$\flat$6)

FCS: (V/*Q*: A$\flat$1) (V/*S*: G1)

FG: (IIc: 2)

FRW(?): V/*S*: E$\flat$1

G: (I: C10)

G with PAPPIER below and to left: V: C2 V: D3 V: F1 V: G2 V: B$\flat$2

GB: (Opus 1)

GF: (I: C7) (I: C10) (I: C14) (I: D6) (I: D7) (I: E$\flat$1) (I: E4) (I: F5) (I: G7) (I: B$\flat$4) (I: B1) (Opus 1^2) (Opus 2) (V: E$\flat$2) (V: F4) (V: A1)

GFA: Opus 1 Opus 2 IV: D2 IV: E$\flat$1 IV: F1 IV: G1

GR: (I: A1)

GR_DG: I: C9

HELLER(?): Opus 2?. *See also* I HELLER(?)
HF: I: C10 (I: D7) Opus 1?
H(?)R: I: D2

IEW: I: C14
IF(?): I: B$\flat$5
IF(HF?): Opus 1
IGF(?): V/*S*: G1
IGS: I: C1 I: C2^2 I: D2^2 I: D8 I: E$\flat$3 I: E$\flat$4^2 I: F6 I: G4 I: A1^2 I: A5 I: A9 I: A11
    I: B$\flat$1 I: B$\flat$8^2 I/*Q*: C2 IIc: 1? IIIc: F2 Opus 1
IHE: I: C7 I: D6 I: F5 I: G7
I HELLER(?): (I: D6) (I: F5) (I: G7) (I: B1) IIIa: F1 IV/*Q*: D1 (IV/*S*: B$\flat$2)
IPR(?): (I: E$\flat$5) (I: A6)
IV: I: C2 I: C11

JRP?: (I: F4?)

LVG: (I: C2) (I: C11)

M: (I: C10) (I: C12) (I: D7) (I: F2) (I: F6) (VIIa: 1)
ML: I: D10 I: B$\flat$6
MM (or MV or MW?): I: C5
MS?: V: C2 V: E$\flat$1 V: B$\flat$2

N(?)? YHE? : (I: A1)

OA?: (V: C2) (V: D1) (V: E$\flat$1) (V: F2) (V: A4) (V: B$\flat$2)
OM: (I: E$\flat$5) (I: G4) (I: B$\flat$3)

P: (I: E1)
PAPPIER: (V: C2) (V: D3) (V: F1) (V: G2) (V: B$\flat$2)
P(?)S: Opus 2

?R? (JRP?): (I: F4)
REAL: (I: C7) (I: D7) (I: F5) (I: F9) (I: G7) (I: B$\flat$4) (I: B1) (Opus 1?) (Opus 1) (Opus 2?)
    (Opus 2^2) (IV: D2) (IV: E$\flat$1) (IV: F1) (IV: G1) (V: F2?) (V: A2?) (V: A2) (VIIa: 2?)
REINF____(?): IV: F4 IV: B$\flat$3 Opus 2
RP(?): (I: E$\flat$5) (I: G4) (I: B$\flat$3)

$B: I: B$\flat$6
$B: V/*Q*: G1

VB (or AB?): Opus 1

W: (I: C8) (I: D4) (I: D7) (I: F2) (I: F6) (I: G3) (Opus 1^3) (Opus 2) (V: C1) (V: C3) (V: D2)
    (V: D3) (V: E$\flat$2) (V: E$\flat$3) (V: F1) (V: F3) (V: G1) (V: G2) (V: A2) (V: A3) (VIIa: 2^2)
WALDS
  ZEL : (V/*Q*: A$\flat$1) (V/*S*: G1)
  FCS
WMS: (Opus 1)

$\frac{ZA}{C}$: (Opus 1^2)

ZEL: (V/*Q*: A$\flat$1) (V/*S*: G1)

NUMBERS

4, WMS below: Opus 1

4 with anchor bottom, ASF(?) below: I: D10 I: B$\flat$6

ORNAMENT. *See also* COAT OF ARMS and EAGLE

Ornament with $\frac{FA}{G}$ below: I: C10

Ornament with F(?)CP below: I: A6 I: B$\flat$3 I: B$\flat$6

Ornament with crescent on top, AF inside: VIIa: 1

Ornament with crown on top and $\frac{AZ}{C}$ inside: I: C9

Ornament with crown on top and W inside: I: F6? Opus 1^3 Opus 2 V: C3 V: D3 V: E$\flat$2 V: F1
   V: G2 V: A3 VIIa: 2^2

Ornament with crown on top and $\frac{ZA}{C}$ inside: Opus 1^2

Ornament with 3 six-pointed stars inside: I: C10 I: C14 I: E$\flat$1 I: E4 Opus 1

Ornament with 3 six-pointed stars inside and crescent on top: I: D7 Opus 1 Opus 2 V: E$\flat$2 V: F4
   V: A1 VIIa: 1

Thin(?) ornament on chain line with F(?) on lower left, C(?) on lower right: I: B$\flat$5 IV: A4 VI: D1 VI: E$\flat$1

PLANT

Plant(?): (I: C8^2) (I: D1) (I: D9) (I: E$\flat$5) (I: F12) (I: G5) (I: A1) (I: A4) (I: A6) (I: A8)

SHIELD

Shield: (I: C2) (I: C11)

STAR(S)

Star: I: C10

Six-pointed star: I: B$\flat$5? (IIc: 1?) (IIIc: F2?)

Star with circle inside: I: A8

Six-pointed(?) star with circle inside: I: C2 I: F6

Six-pointed star within six-pointed(?) star: I: E4 Opus 1

3 six-pointed stars: (I: C10) (I: C14) (I: D7) (Opus 1^2) (Opus 2) (V: E$\flat$2) (V: F4) (V: A1) (VIIa: 1)

SWORDS, CROSSED

Crossed swords: I: C5? I: D6

Crossed keys or crossed swords: I: C7 I: F5 I: B$\flat$4 IIa: 1 Opus 2?

WHEEL

Wheel with baldachin on top, AFC below: I: E$\flat$1 I: B$\flat$5

MISCELLANEOUS ELEMENTS

$\circ$C : I: E$\flat$3 I: E$\flat$4 I: E1 I: F1 I: G5 I: A6 I: B$\flat$5

4P with FG below: IIc: 2

Double chain lines: I: C13 I: D3 I: E2 I: F3 I: G1 I: A2 IIIa: F1 Opus 2 IV: C1 IV: C2
   IV: D1 IV: D2 IV: D3 IV: E$\flat$1 IV: F1 IV: F2 IV: G1 IV: G3 IV: A2 IV: B$\flat$4

INDEX OF COPYISTS

Reference is made to the catalog number of a work which has a listed copy attributed to the copyist or copyist group. Exponents refer to the number of copies with this attribution under the given catalog number. An asterisk to the left of the name of the copyist or copyist group indicates a facsimile is included in the section **FACSIMILES OF SELECTED COPYISTS.**

COPY SHOPS

*Group A   Professional Viennese copy shop which included Landon's Viennese Copyist No. 2. *See* **ANONYMOUS COPYISTS**

I: C1 I: $C2^2$ I: C5 I: $C8^3$ I: C10 I: C12 I: D1 I: $D2^2$ I: D4 I: D5 I: D7 I: D8 I: D9 I: $E^\flat 1$ I: $E^\flat 3$ I: $E^\flat 4^3$ I: $E^\flat 5^3$ I: F1 I: $F2^2$ I: F4 I: $F6^2$ I: F8 I: F11 I: F12 I: G2 I: G3 I: $G4^2$ I: G5 I: G8 I: $A1^3$ I: A4 I: A5 I: $A6^3$ I: A7 I: A8 I: A10 I: A11 I: $B^\flat 1$ I: $B^\flat 2^2$ I: $B^\flat 3$ I: $B^\flat 6$ I: $B^\flat 8$ I/Q: C2

*Group B   Professional Italian copyists perhaps working together in Vienna or northern Italy. (For a further facsimile, *see Joseph Haydn Werke*, III/1.)

I: $E^\flat 3$ I: $E^\flat 4$ I: E1 I: F1 I: G5 I: A6 Opus 1 Opus 2 V: C1 V: C3 V: D2 V: D3 V: $E^\flat 2$ V: $E^\flat 3$ V: F1 V: F3 V: G1 V: G2 V: A2 V: A3

IDENTIFIED COPYISTS (SIGNED COPIES)

*N. H.   Professional Viennese copyist who during the last two decades of the eighteenth century copied a large number of chamber works now in the **A-Wn**-Kaisersammlung. (For a further facsimile, *see* Kirkendale/FUGE.)

IIIc: $E^\flat 2$ Opus 1 Opus 2 IV: C1 IV: C2 IV: D1 IV: D2 IV: D3 IV: $E^?1$ IV: F1 IV: F2 IV: G1 IV: G3 IV: A2 IV: $B^\flat 4$

Simon Haschke   *See* Viennese Copyist No. 6 under **ANONYMOUS COPYISTS**

P. Leandri	Director of the school of the Benedictine Abbey at Göttweig in Niederösterreich from 1759-1768.
	I: C1 I: F7 I: A6 I: B$\flat$3 I: B$\flat$6 IIIc: F2
Joseph Los	Copyist at the Cistercian Abbey Osek near Dux (Duchcov) in Bohemia.
	I: D10
P. Marianus	Regens Chori at Göttweig Abbey in Niederösterreich from 1773-1813.
	I: F4
P. Maurus	Copyist at the Benedictine Abbey at Raigern (Rajhrad) in Moravia.
	I: B$\flat$4
Francesco Nigst	Esterházy copyist who also served as accountant and violinist from 1760-1772. (*See* Larsen/HÜB, pp. 71-72, and Bartha/BRIEFE, pp. 62-64.)
	I: B$\flat$8
Carlo d'Ordonez	VIIa: 1
*Johann Schmutzer	Professional Viennese copyist (= Viennese No. 4?). (For further references, *see* Brown/CHAMBER, p. 226, n. 29.)
	I: C13 I: D3 I: E2 I: F3 I: G1 I: A2 Opus 2
Franz Sparry	Regens Chori at Kremsmünster Abbey from 1747-1767.
	I/*Q*: C1
Speer	Kapellmeister to the Clam-Gallas family.
	I: C10
Francisci Caroli Stuckler	Apparently a monk at Stift Villingen in southern Germany.
	I: A8

ANONYMOUS COPYISTS†

*Viennese Copyist No. 1	I: B$\flat$3 VI: D1 VI: E$\flat$1
*Viennese Copyist No. 2	A member of Group A. *See* **COPY SHOPS**
*Viennese Copyist No. 4	(= Johann Schmutzer?)
	I: C7 I: D6^2 I: E$\flat$1 I: F5 I: G7 I: B$\flat$4 I: B$\flat$5^2 I: B1 IIa: 1 Opus 1 Opus 2 IV/*Q*: D1
*Viennese Copyist No. 5	Opus 1^2
*Viennese Copyist No. 6	Possibly Simon Haschke. (*See* Brown/CHAMBER, p. 228.)
	I: C2? I: F6? IV: F4? IV: B$\flat$3? Opus 2? V: B$\flat$1 V/*Q*: G1 V/*Q*: A$\flat$1 V/*S*: E$\flat$1
*Viennese Copyist No. 7	Executed a series of copies now located at **I-Fc**.
	I: C7 I: C10 I: C14 I: E$\flat$1 I: E4 I: F5 I: G7 I: B$\flat$4 I: B1

---

† In Landon/ SYMPHONIES, p. 611, three professional Viennese copyists are defined by number. Copyists Nos. 4-7 above are the editor's additions to Landon's series.